# Tamara

## Revenge of a Catholic Schoolboy

Victor Edmundo Villaseñor

20 June 14

# Quotes

"I know God will not give me anything I can't handle. I just wish that He didn't have so much trust in me."
*Mother Teresa of Calcutta*

"There will come a time when you believe everything is finished. That will be the beginning."
*Louis L'Amour*

"Whatever you can do or dream you can do, begin it. Boldness has genius, power, and magic.
*Johann Wolfgang van Goethe*

"Row, Row, Row your Boat, Gently down the Stream, Merrily, Merrily, Merrily Life is but a Dream!"
*Confucius*

"Before civilization you, me, we, all of us were like weeds, because a civilized plant like a rose you got to feed and water and spray for bugs or it will die. But a wild uncivilized plant like a weed, you don't give it nothing and it lives. You poison it and it comes back the following year with the rains. You pour cement over it and it will break that concrete reaching for the sunlight of God.

And this is how we, humans, all used to be all over the earth. Uncivilized and wild of heart and alive of soul and indestructible as we reached for the Light of God!"

*Juan Salvador Villaseñor*

# Definitions

**From the Webster's New World Dictionary pre-1990:**

**Genius:** guardian deity, or spirit of a person; spirit, natural ability. According to ancient Roman belief, a guardian spirit is assigned to a person at birth.

**Catholic:** universal, all-inclusive; of general interest or value; hence, having broad sympathies or understanding; liberal.

**Balance:** an instrument for weighing, especially one that opposes equal weights, as in two matched scales hanging from either end of a lever supported exactly in the middle. The imaginary scales of fortune or fate, as an emblem of justice or the power to decide; hence, the power to decide human fate, value, etc. A state of bodily equilibrium: as he kept his balance on the tightrope. Equilibrium in design, painting, music composition, harmonious proportions. The constellation Libra, or the seventh sign of the zodiac.

**God:** Any of various beings as conceived as supernatural, immortal, and having special powers over the lives and affairs of people, and of course nature. An image that is worshipped. In monotheistic religions, the creator and ruler of the universal, regarded as eternal, infinite, all-powerful, and all-knowing; Supreme Being; Almighty.

**Miracle**: an event or action that apparently contradicts known scientific laws, and is hence thought to be due to supernatural causes, especially to an act of God. A remarkable event or thing. A marvel.

**Leprechaun:** Irish Folklore of a fairy in the form of a little old man who can reveal hidden treasure to anyone who catches him.

**From the Southwest Native American Elders:**

**Stick People:** The spirit of our ancestors come back to us after dark in the form of little stick people, and if we are pure of heart they give us health and treasure, but if we are not pure of heart they can be detrimental to the health of the Song of Our Soul. For all of us come into this world with Our Own Song gifted to us by the Holy Creator.

# Introduction

A few years back I was babysitting Erik, my sister Linda's youngest son, and I took him to the beach. He was a big, strong, blond Viking-looking little Mexican kid of maybe four years old. I didn't realize he'd never seen the ocean before, and we went down by the Oceanside pier. It was low tide. There were a lot of quick long-legged shore birds working the incoming and outgoing little waves.

Screeching with *gusto*, Erik ran out to get the birds and when they flew away, he saw the sea was also pulling away from him, so he ran after the little waves, laughing with joy. But then when he saw that the waves had stopped running away from him, and they'd gathered together into even larger waves, and they were now coming back towards him in a rush of crashing sound and speed, he turned and ran as fast as he could and got behind me.

Oh, he was all out of breath and his little heart was beating fast, but then when he saw the waves weren't going to get him and were instead going back out again, he picked up a rock and chased after the waves. And this time when the waves stopped going out and gathered together to come back towards the shore, what did he do? He didn't run away from the waves like last time. No, he stood his ground like a little long haired blond Mexican Viking and threw his rock at the oncoming water with a scream of defiance! But to his shock the incoming waves weren't affected by his mighty throw and they still came rushing towards him just like before, so he turned to run, but it was too late and the waves knocked him face down into the sand.

I laughed and he leaped up, all wet and terrified and ran behind me, then once he felt he was safe, he cursed at the sea with all his might. There were dozens of people around us, who'd been watching and laughing along with me, but now they stopped grinning when they heard the little boy curse, and they looked at me with disapproval.

"Hey, he's not my kid," I said. "He's my sister's child. I didn't know he even knew those words."

Giving me a look like, "Yeah, sure, buddy," they all moved away from me, and this time when waters went out again, my nephew picked up two rocks to run after the sea. But then when he saw the waves gather before him once again, he didn't throw his two stones. No, he just dropped them and turned, running back as fast as he could and got behind me before he could get knocked down into the sand again.

Smiling, I reached down and picked him up into my arms, and now that he was feeling safe way up high above the little waves, what did he do? A gleam of joy came to his eyes and he began cursing at the sea once again. I started laughing and laughing, and yet I also realized that he needed to learn what was going on, so I took him back up to higher ground and sat down with him on the dry sand.

"Look," I said to him, "see way over there to the right how the waves also come in and then look, look, they go back out, too. Do you see that?"

"Yes," he said.

"Good," I said, "and now look way over here to the left and see how the waves also come in and then go out." He looked and nodded. "Good, and now look as far as you can see in both directions, to the right and to the left, and see that the same thing is happening over and over again in both directions for as far as you can see."

His eyes lit up. He saw it. He really did.

"Excellent," I said. "Now look back and see that these waves directly in front of us do the same thing." He looked. "Good," I said, rubbing his shoulder affectionately. "Now can you understand that maybe, just maybe these waves in front of us were never really out to get you or anything like that? They were just doing what waves do. Can you see that?" He nodded vigorously. "Good. Very good. So now, in life, the whole thing is to not just look at what's in front of you, but to always look left and right before you cross the street, when you play ball, when you do almost anything, so you can then see the larger picture about what's going on. Does this make sense?" He nodded. "Good. Now go out and have fun, knowing that these waves, and life itself are not out to get you or even against you. Go! Go! Have fun!"

He nodded, then like the true little brave Mexican Viking that he was, he leaped up and with great joy and a whole new perspective, he ran at the waves again, but this time he turned and headed back away from them before they got him. He'd learned. He really had, and so now he could have all the fun he wanted and not get knocked down anymore.

And this is exactly what this book *Revenge of a Catholic Schoolboy* is about, because the time has come in our "Godelution" for all of us, Collectively, to start accessing the "Kingdom of God" that Jesus so wisely told us is within each of us, then *bingo!* just like my nephew Erik, we can begin to see the much larger picture of what's going on all about us and have fun without resorting to fear and violence.

You see, according to the Mayan Calendar, our Mother Earth has been working for eons of timeless time in increments of 26,000 years just like the incoming and outgoing waves. And presently we have just finished up 26,000 years of aggressive global male energy and are now moving into 26,000 years of compassionate global female energy. In other words, there's nothing we can do to stop world harmony and peace and abundance for all, because it comes to us every 26,000 years. And this isn't a farfetched dream, but the larger, much larger, picture of reality with which I was raised by my Yaqui Indian grandmother.

In fact, every evening my Yaqui Indian *mamagrande* would rock me in her old wooden rocking chair by her outhouse under the big avocado tree in the old Mexican *barrio* of Carlsbad, California, and she'd point up at the stars telling me that the stars were our *familia,* and that our beloved Mother Earth belonged to Six Sister Planets.

"You see, *mijito,*"she'd tell me as she took my little legs and arms in hand, "we Human People are all five-pointed Walking Stars. Two legs," she'd say, tickling my legs, "two arms," she'd say, tickling my arms, "and one head," she'd say, tickling my neck and head, and I'd screech and giggle and laugh, and she'd then explain to me that each of us came across the Heavens gathering Stardust so we could help *Papito Dios*, little Daddy God, plant His ongoing Sacred Holy Garden of Heaven on Mother Earth.

"You see," she'd tell me, "God needs us as much as we need God, and so this is why He sent us along with our very own Guardian Angel so we Human People would be sure to get our earthly work done."

And so this was how I was raised for the first five years of my life . . . with my *mamagrande* explaining to me all the wonders of the Universe and that little Daddy God needed us Human People as much as we needed Him. For we were all five-pointed Walking Stars who'd come across the Universe with our own Guardian Angel, gathering Stardust so we could then help *Papito Dios* plant His ongoing Holy Garden of Heaven on Earth.

So, dear reader, now please fasten your seatbelt and let's you and me take a "VoyageDream" of Cellular Memory past the Mother Moon and to the Furthest Stars within our very own "Kingdom of God" . . . Back To The Future when we were All, All, All Indigenous People the whole world over, and we All Knew our Original Instructions. Truly, understand that for all of us back then the question had never been is there intelligent life on other planets. The real question had always been when is there going to be intelligent life on this planet? Ready? So let's go back to "yesteryear" when we Human People all lived within the larger picture, and so we were all full of wonder and magic, and happiness! BIG BIG HAPPINESS!

Thank you, *gracias*,

Victor E. Villaseñor

P.S. *Revenge of a Catholic Schoolboy* is the first book of a trilogy. The second volume is titled *Walking in Beauty* and the third is titled *Dancing Stars!*

# BOOK ONE

# One

I was shocked.

A group of retired nuns and priests were inviting me
to go and speak to them up by the Great Lakes near the
Canadian border, but I didn't want to go. I mean, I hadn't
written that well about the Catholic Church in my book
*Rain of Gold,* and yet it was this very book that had caused
these old nuns and priests to write to me. I decided to sleep
on the matter as my dad had always done whenever he'd
had an important decision to make, and in the morning,
much to my surprise, I awoke with the realization that I
still had a lot of love and even some good memories of
the Church.

In fact, looking back I could now see that it had been
the sounds and smells that had first caused me to fall
in love with the Holy Roman Catholic Church. I'd just
been a little kid, and the smell of the smoking incense,
and the quiet sounds of the people praying, and the old
deaf priest's large booming voice full of warm sing-song
sounding-language, and then the altar boys singing back
to the priest with beautiful high-sounding voices, pretending to also be speaking in Latin, but in actuality they'd be
singing to the old priest in Spanish, telling him that they
agreed with him and it was best to cook the wild turkey
in Mexican green sauce. Oh, it had all been so much fun.
The old priest dressed up in an elaborate dress like a

queen and chanting with such seriousness, and the altar boys, also dressed in elaborate dresses, chanting back to him with so much *gusto*.

"*Gua-jo-lote! Co-cido en sal-saaa verrr-de!*" would chant the altar boys, and most parents would get mad, hearing that the boys were tricking the half-deaf old priest, but my dad would join us kids and sing along with the laughing, giggling altar boys.

Oh, it was the best show in town and these first wonderful memories began for me at Saint Patrick's Holy Catholic Church in the Mexican *barrio* of Carlsbad, California with the smell of burning incense being whirled about in a little silver bell, and the quiet rolling whispers of my mother and grandmother saying the rosary. Then, when I got a little older, it was the bells of Saint Mary's Star of the Sea in Oceanside, a few miles north from the *barrio* of Carlsbad, with which I fell in love. The loud-clanging bells, and the smell of the sea mixed with cutting flowers and incense, slightly different smells than the ones in Carlsbad, but the sounds of the people praying were exactly the same and wonderful.

Then came the San Luis Rey Mission, king of all the missions of California, with its great towering bell that could be heard across the whole valley full of luscious green fields and best of all the hundreds of beautiful goldfish in the water fountain right across from the entrance of the huge magnificent great-smelling mission where, on some lucky Sundays, we got to see wild pigeons flying about inside of the church as the old priest and the altar boys chanted back and forth to each other about the best way to cook wild turkey in Mexican green sauce.

And also, looking back, I could now see that it had felt very *especial* to get all dressed up every Sunday and listen to the sounds of the Holy Roman Catholic Church, and then get to go out for breakfast as one big happy hungry *familia* who'd confessed our sins, received Holy Communion, and were now all at peace with God Almighty, the Holy Creator of the whole Universe!

But still, for days, I procrastinated, because I just couldn't see myself going to see a bunch of retired nuns and priests. Hell, I could also still remember all the abuses that I'd received at Catholic school. What happened was that I'd been going to public school in South Oceanside just a few blocks from our home and everything had been going . . . well, not too bad, until I got to the third grade, then I just couldn't seem to be able to learn how to read.

I mean, reading in second grade had been difficult enough for me, but reading in third grade had just been beyond my comprehension. School became a nightmare. The kids began making fun of me. I became a bed wetter. And I flunked the third grade, but I was also told not to worry, that by taking the third grade over, I'd surely learn how to read. But I didn't, and this was when even my best friends began to call me stupid and explained to me that it was because I was a Mexican.

Then I flunked the third grade for a second time, and kids began to throw rocks at me and wait for me after school so they could beat me up. I got mad and would grab and bite and scratch the kids and my parents were called in and my teacher told them that I was always getting into fights. And this was when my parents told my teacher to pass me on to the fourth grade, and they'd then take me out of public school and put me in Catholic school out at the San Luis Rey Mission.

At first the teacher said she couldn't do that, but then when my dad leaned in so close to her with his big smoking cigar and a lug of avocados with an envelope full of money, my teacher's eyes got so big with fear that she quickly agreed to pass me on. Then driving home my mother explained that the nuns and priests weren't Protestants and so they'd be kinder and more patient with me and so I'd be sure to learn how to read.

And my mom and dad were almost right, because Sister Theresa, the little nun who was assigned to teach me how to read after school, was wonderful and kind and never got mad at me when I didn't get it. Within a week I was in love with her and so one afternoon I asked her if she would marry me when I grew up.

She smiled, I'll never forget, and took my hand and explained to me that she was already married to Jesus.

"He's dead, you know," I said.

"Yes, but I'm married to Our Lord Jesus in spirit," she said, still smiling.

"Oh, that's okay," I said, "we can then get married in body and have babies."

But she was never able to give me her answer, because just then the big, old mother superior came crashing through the door, screaming at me that I was the devil and slapped me so hard that she knocked me out of my chair, and then she went after my little nun, slapping her and slapping her. And this was when Sister Theresa's habit was knocked off of her head, and I saw that her long, beautiful dark red hair was the same color as my horse's mane and tail. And she was so young and beautiful and yet she wouldn't fight back or defend herself, and the big, old mother superior just kept hitting her.

This incident I would never forget. I'd only been eight years old, but still I'd been so full of love that I'd leaped up off the floor and attacked the smelly old mother superior, getting under her long robe and biting her leg and gouging my nails into her soft flesh. She screamed bloody murder and quit hitting my little nun and began hitting me on the head. But still I continued biting her until the priest came rushing in and grabbed me by my hair and dragged me down the hallway, then locked me in a broom closet. After that, I was never allowed to see my little nun again, and when months later I did see her, her face instantly filled with terror and she took off running.

My heart died. What had they done to her? And also after that incident, it was like the old mother superior and the priest now thought that they had an open license to beat me and after each beating explain to me that I'd been born with Original Sin, and so it was their sworn duty and for the good of my soul for them to beat me and keep me away from all the other kids.

And so no, no, no, now as an adult I couldn't see myself going to see any old, retired nuns and priests. After all, what I'd written about in *Rain of Gold* was that God was full of *amor*. Not wrath. And that every day was *otro milagro de Dios*, every day was another miracle given to us by God, and that our job here on Mother Earth was for us, five-pointed Walking Stars, to help Our Holy Creator plant His ongoing Sacred Garden of Heaven on Earth.

But then finally, after a few days of still not being able to make up my mind, I decided to just go across the grass, past the chicken coops, and see my mother who lived in our new, smaller house. My dad had passed over ten years ago, and so I now spoke to my mother, who was almost 90 years old, but she'd never been much of a talker like my dad. To go to church and pray her rosary had always been more of my mother's style of how to deal with difficult situations. Getting to her house, her front door was open, which was okay. At our little *rancho* in South Oceanside we hardly ever locked our doors at night, and during the day we didn't close them half of the time.

"*Mama*," I called out as I went inside, "I'd like to speak with you."

"Okay," she called back, "I'm in the kitchen. I'm making myself a *quesadilla*. Would you like one?"

I'd already had breakfast about two hours ago, but still the thought of having one of my mother's delicious *quesadillas*, meaning a handmade *tortilla* folded in half with cheese in the middle, sounded pretty good.

"Yeah, sure," I said, licking my lips. "Do you also have avocado? I can go and pick a couple if you'd like."

"No, I already picked a few this morning," she said. "You slice one while I do the *quesadillas* on the *comal*."

"Okay," I said, and so I washed my hands, dried them, then began feeling the avocados to see which one was the ripest.

Sitting down with my mother, we ate our *quesadillas* with fresh slices of avocado and homemade *salsa*, then I came right to the point.

"*Mama*," I said, "I've been invited to go to Wisconsin up by the Great Lakes to give a talk to a bunch of old retired nuns and priests, but I don't know if I can go."

"Oh, you don't think you have warm enough clothes?" she said. "Well, that's no problem, *mijito*. Just do as your father always said he learned to do up in Montana and wear many layers. You'll be okay, *mijito*. Don't worry."

"*Mama*, I got the clothes. That's not the *problema*," I said. "The *problema* is that I was well, you know, abused by the nuns and priests out at the San Luis Rey Mission so much that part of me just doesn't want to go."

"But didn't you bite a nun? Isn't that what started the whole problem?"

"Oh, *mama*," I said, "I've told you a thousand times that that's not how it happened."

"Well, the priest, he told your father and me that you bit a nun so hard that they'd had to take her to the hospital."

"*Mama*, please stop it! You just don't know what happened, and every time I've tried to explain, you twist things all around."

"Well, okay, maybe I do," she said, "but let's be practical and realize that all those things happened to you a long time ago, *mijito*, and you're now a grown man with a wife and kids. Do you think your father and I could have succeeded in this country if we'd held onto all the bad things that happened to us? Oh, no, *mijito*, we all got to let go and keep going. That's our only hope," she said, making the sign of the cross over herself and adding the words, "*con el favor de Dios.*" Meaning, with the blessing of God.

"Yes, *mama*, I can see that that's true," I said, taking in a deep breath, and I almost said 'but if this was really true, then why have you held onto so many bad things all these years?' But I didn't need to say this. It was my mother who now, looking at me in the eyes, said it best.

"And I also know, *mijito*, that I haven't always been a very good example of doing this," she said. "After all, it was your father, not me," she added, "who went to see Doctor

Hoskins when he was sick and dying of cancer. I couldn't do that. In fact, it enraged me that your father would do such a thing, because it had been that no good drunken doctor's fault that your brother Joseph died! Oh, he was the only doctor in town back then, and he caused so many deaths because of his stupid, drunken ways!"

She stopped and tears came to her eyes, and I took in another deep breath. I, too, remembered my brother's death very well. Joseph had been 16 years old and I'd been eight years old and he'd been my best friend. Oh, if he had lived I don't think that I would have flunked the third grade for a second time, because he'd always had a way of teaching me how to do things with such patience and good natural horse sense. In fact, he was the one who'd taught me how to play marbles and, with his teachings, I became the marble champion of my whole school.

"And yet looking back," continued my mother, "I'm beginning to now see how your father was able to do that, because, well, I'm approaching the end of my life, *mijito*, so I . . . I can now see that if we don't show forgiveness, then how can we expect God to show us forgiveness when we pass over?" And it was now my mother who took in a big, deep breath. "*Mijito*, you've got to go and see those nuns and priests," she added. "Truly, it will help you, yourself, deep inside of your heart and soul."

"Oh, *mama*," I said.

"You say that they are old retired nuns and priests, right?"

"Yes," I said.

"Well, then, remember what happened to your little sister Teresita when the old dying nun asked to see her?"

"Remind me," I said.

"Well, they called me from Saint Mary's Star of the Sea and said that one of the nuns' old helpers was in the hospital dying and she wanted to see your little sister. I took Teresita, and the sick old woman called your sister to her bedside, but she refused to go near the old lady."

"How old was Sita at the time?" I asked. Most of us never called our youngest sister Teresita. We called her Sita for short and she liked it.

"She was about, well, I guess, maybe ten. And the woman begged her to come close, but you know how your sister is when she sets her mind to something."

My mother was absolutely right. Our little sister could be strong as iron.

"Well, finally, the sick old woman said, 'Child, in the name of God, could you please forgive me for how I treated you all these years.'"

"I remember now," I said. "Sita shook her head, telling her no, that she would not forgive her, and she walked out of the room."

"Yes, exactly," said my mother, taking in another deep breath, "and I saw that old sick woman's face fill with fear, and all the nuns around her tried to console her, telling her that she'd been a very good person, but none of this helped. It was like, well, I guess, she was seeing hell itself deep inside of herself."

I nodded. "Yes, she probably was, *mama*." And this was going to be tough, but I wasn't going to chicken out. "And do you remember who Sita was even more mad at than . . . than at that old nun's helper?" I asked.

"No, tell me."

"You, *mama*," I said with tears bursting from my eyes. "You! Because during all those years of abuse you never once believed Sita! You always believed the nuns and that nun's old helper!"

"That's true," said my mother with tears also bursting from her eyes.

"Yeah, you'd thought that Sita had made it all up, just like you'd thought Linda and I had made up all our stuff about the nuns and priests."

"That's true, that's true," said my mother. "But how could I think differently? Those nuns would talk to your father and me with such respect and kindness, and . . . and they'd dedicated their whole lives for the love of God and the good of humanity, so how could we believe that those same nuns and their helpers could be so abusive? It just didn't make sense, *mijito*."

"OH, *MAMA*," I yelled with my heart pounding, "AND THIS IS EXACTLY why I don't want to go to speak to those old nuns and priests! Am I just going to pretend that everything is Jim Dandy okay? Or am I going to be blunt and ask these old nuns and priests how many of them slapped kids, pulled their hair, and sneaked into the boys' bathroom, trying to see if they were touching themselves, so they could then scream at them that they were GOING TO GO TO HELL AND BURN FOR ETERNITY!

"Can't you understand, *mama*, that it was no accident that these nuns and priests knew how to handle you guys. We, your kids, came into this world with Original Sin and all that crap, so we couldn't be trusted, and you, the adults, had your own daily ongoing sins, and so you couldn't trust yourselves, either, and so these nuns and priests had us all by the balls, trained to divide and conquer our *familia* just like armies divide and conquer nations. This is what Cortez did to Mexico. His little group of soldiers could have never won if they hadn't been experts at manipulation and deception!

"Truly, I'm now beginning to realize that a lot of nuns and priests don't even believe in Jesus or in God. What they really believe in is . . . is the survival of their institution, and in keeping all the power in their own hands, so they can then accumulate huge amounts of wealth for their diocese and the Pope!"

"Oh, *mijito*, do you really believe this?"

"Absolutely! Look at all the gold they stole from the New World. And you, more than most people, should know this, because you were born in a gold mining town in Mexico."

"But those were Americans who were taking the gold."

"Yes, but before the Americans it was Spain and the Church who raped all of the Americas! Let's not kid ourselves, *mama*, it's been the Church who's been backing up the rich for centuries, so they can get their share of the spoils. Can't you see that, *mama*? You and *papa* were adults and you were rich on top of that and . . . and . . . extremely generous with your donations, so of course, they spoke to you with respect and kindness. Truly, *mama*, I just don't know how I can possibly go to see these old nuns and priests without WANTING TO RIP THEIR HEARTS OUT! And bluntly tell them what I really think of their manipulating, abusive ways?"

I stopped and took in a great big deep breath. "Oh, *mama*," I now said more gently, "I'll never forget how I climbed over that wall to go looking for my little nun and when I saw her sitting in the rose garden reading her Bible and I went up to her, she smiled at first, but then her whole face twisted into terror and she ran away from me in fear." The tears were streaming down my face. "What did they do to my beautiful, kind little nun, *mama?* She must've been no more than eighteen years old, and she . . . she was the first teacher I ever had who was kind to me and didn't look down her nose at me when I didn't get it. Truly, I wish I'd bitten that smelly old mother superior's leg completely off!"

"*Mijito,* how can you talk like this?"

"Easy, *mama,* easy," I said, wiping the tears off my face with the back of my hand, "it used to enrage me the way they'd always talk to you and *papa.* They're all great actors. All the nuns and priests. And the best actors among them become the bishops and cardinals and mother superiors. I swear, they really got their pious little mannerisms down to a science. Remember how that old head nun out at the mission so quickly changed her whole way that first day when you slipped her that envelope full of money across the desk? Suddenly she couldn't do enough for us, and she became all smiles and told you that yes, of course, they'd be most happy to accept me and assign a nun to help teach me how to read after school.

"And then when that little young nun was so kind and nice to me that I fell in love with her and asked her if she would marry me when I got big, what did that old smelly nun do? She, who, I guess, had been outside of our door listening the whole time, came bursting into our room, slapped me across the face so hard that she knocked me out of my chair, called me the devil, and then she began slapping my little nun. And, *mama,* Sister Theresa wouldn't fight back or even try to protect herself," I said with tears pouring down my face. "So this was when I leaped up off the floor and began biting the big old nun so she WOULDN'T KILL MY LOVING, KIND LITTLE NUN!" I added with a shout.

My mother was stunned. "But why didn't you tell us all this years ago? All we knew was that you'd bit a nun and they'd had to take her to the hospital."

"I tried, *mama,*" I said. "I really tried to tell you, but I just couldn't find the words because I was a child, *a*nd they'd convinced me that I was evil and Mexican and sub-human. Truly, they were even worse to me than they'd been in public school when the teachers allowed the kids to keep making fun of me because I couldn't learn to read."

My mother reached into her pocket and brought out her hand embroidered handkerchief with the little pink flowers and green leaves, which she had embroidered while she and my dad watched T.V. together, and she handed it to me. I took the pretty little handkerchief and dried my eyes.

"Oh, *mijito,*" she said, taking in a couple of great big, deep breaths, "it just seems to me that your father and I were so busy trying to be successful in this country that we failed as parents for you kids. Your older sister Tencha, just a young innocent girl and getting pregnant, or maybe even raped and having a child out of wedlock, and us being so ashamed and trying to keep up appearances that we quickly got her out of town and put her in a home down in San Diego where no one would know her. And then your brother, not liking football because he was so gentle, but still he played with all his heart so he, too, could fit in at school, and the coaches kept egging him on to keep playing until he injured himself. And then when we took him to see Dr. Hoskins, what did that no good drunk say, 'He only has growing pains, so keep him playing.'"

Tears came to my mother's eyes. "And your father and I could see that there was something very wrong with your brother, but we believed Dr. Hoskins because he was an American doctor, and we were too busy doing business to pay much attention. And it wasn't until the new young doctor named Pace came to town, who'd just gotten out of the Navy, that he took just one look at your brother and rushed him to Scripps Hospital in La Jolla. But it was too late. His football injuries had turned to yellow jaundice, injuries that could have been so easily taken care of at an earlier stage. Oh, we failed, *mijito!*" said my mother, with tears pouring down her face. "Your father and I, we failed all of you children!"

"Oh, *mama,*" I said, handing her back her embroidered handkerchief, "it's not you and *papa* who failed. It's this whole system in which we live that has failed all of us."

"What do you mean?" she said, drying her eyes.

"Look, Doctor Hoskin's license should have been revoked years ago, *mama,* and nuns and priests should never have been allowed and even encouraged to be abusive. You see, it's the very structure of these old out-of-date, male-based institutions that are failing us, the people, because they're full of secrecy, control, and have no real love and respect for ordinary people.

"Think about it, *mama,* the foundation of the Catholic Church is based on the . . . the concept of an all-male angry god who's full of wrath, and then we're told that we humans come into this world with Original Sin, so this then tells the Church to treat all of us as basically evil, and hence gives them the right to be abusive. Can you see that? It's an all male-based set up so that then a few old impotent men can . . . can manipulate all of us with ease.

So, then, your failure wasn't your failure, *mama*. You and *papa* were always very wise good people, *mama*, because both of you were raised by your Indigenous Indian mothers who were towers of faith and strength and believed in a kind, loving God who was both male and female."

"Well," she said, looking at me in a new way, "if this is what you really think, then maybe this is exactly what you should go and tell these retired nuns and priests."

"Are you kidding? This is what got me slapped until I was bloody out at the mission, *mama*! Priests and nuns don't want to hear about any of this!"

"Yes, I'm sure that was true," she said. "But these nuns and priests have read your book, and so maybe they're minds have opened up."

"That would be a miracle," I said.

"Yes," she said, "and did we not raise you kids to understand that every day is, in fact, *otro milagro* given to us by God?"

I nodded. "Yes, that is how you raised us, *mama*," I said. "And this is also what I have been writing about all these years."

I stopped and breathed and my mother and I kept looking at each other. My dad had done this, too, and it was called eye gazing, which, according to Native People, was a Sacred Form of Heart to Heart Soul Touching. I pushed back in my chair and got to my feet. I'd never expected to get into such a deep conversation with my mother. It was almost as if the Spirit of my dad had come into her now that he was on the Other Side of Living and she, too, had become a great talker.

"You're right, *mama*," I said, "they have read *Rain of Gold*. That's why they've contacted me, so maybe they will be open for me to tell them what I really think and feel. But, oh, no, *mama*," I added, shaking my head, "I don't know if I can do this! Not when I can't get it out of my head all the horrors that the Church has done! Hell, the Catholic Church alone, mostly through Spain and Portugal, slaughtered well over 60 to 80 million Native Americans in the name of God! And not just the men, but the women and children, too, like they slaughtered your mother's own Yaqui people, *mama*! And damnit, nobody knows anything about this! Hell, what the Germans did to the Jews is small potatoes compared to what the Church has done worldwide! *Papa* knew this, and he wasn't afraid to admit it!"

"Yes," she said, with tears once more coming to her eyes, "and your father is also the one who found it in his heart to go and . . . and forgive the man who was responsible for your brother's untimely death. He was only 16 years old," she added, "only 16, and still your father was able to forgive."

Hearing this, I now stopped all my talking and took my mother into my arms. I, too, remembered what my dad had done very well. I'd been about 17 years old and going to the Army Navy Academy in Carlsbad where my brother Joseph had also gone and that day I'd just gotten home from school when I found out that my dad had driven up California Street to see Dr. Hoskins. My mother had been screaming with rage and she'd demanded for me to get in our ranch truck and drive after my dad and stop him from seeing the doctor. But I hadn't wanted to get involved. Yet seeing my mother so angry, and she was normally such a calm person, I'd finally agreed to do what she asked and I'd gotten into our old ranch truck and drove after my dad.

And I'd gotten there just as my dad was walking past the corrals to where Dr. Hoskins was in his riding ring with one of his Tennessee Walkers. I'll never forget, watching my dad in his big western hat walking up to the doctor in his English gear. Both of them were old, distinguished-looking grey-haired men. I watched the doctor dismount and take off his right-hand glove to shake my dad's hand.

Then I couldn't believe it. My dad was actually accepting the hand of the man who was responsible for my brother Joseph's death. I quickly turned to leave, but this was when my dad spotted me and waved me to come over so he could introduce me to this man that I'd avoided all of my life. I didn't know what to do, but my dad insisted and so I finally walked over, feeling like a traitor to my brother and mother.

"This is our other son, Edmundo," said my dad. My parents always called me by my middle name Edmundo at home.

My eyes flashed with rage and the doctor saw it, but still he reached out to take my hand. And what did I do? I couldn't believe it, I, too, reached out and took his hand, but if he had so much as squeezed my hand just a little bit, I would've jerked him to me and side stepped him, slamming him to the ground as we did at our wrestling workouts every afternoon at the Academy. But he didn't squeeze my hand like a lot of old men do trying to show that they still have power. No, he shook my hand with such gentleness that in his own way he was saying he . . . he was sorry. So I didn't slam him, but still I quickly took my hand back and just stood there listening. And my dad and the old doctor spoke about horses and the price of hay and not one single word was ever mentioned about my brother. And yet before my dad and I left, I could see in both of these old men's eyes that a peace had been made between them, and that the doctor, who was now himself dying of cancer, was truly grateful that my dad had come to see him. I took in several deep breaths, remembering all this.

"Okay, *mama*," I finally said, "maybe you're right, and I should go and see these old retired nuns and priests. But truly, I don't know what I'll do when I get there."

"You will pray, *mijito*, you will pray and ask God for guidance, and then you will know what to do, and who knows, this . . . this might end up being the most important talk of your life."

"What? Why would you say this, *mama*?"

"Because, *mijito*, over and over again your father and I found in business here in the United States, that that which we really didn't want to do was often the very thing that caused us to learn the most and grow the most."

"Well, yes, but this isn't business."

"Oh, isn't the business of religion the biggest business in all the world? You, yourself, spoke of this only moments ago."

I nodded. "Yes, I guess you're right."

"Look, *mijito*, your father never wanted to stop bootlegging, but then when he was forced to stop because prohibition was over and we got that pool hall from Archie in Carlsbad and we went legal, our whole life changed in a way that we'd never dreamed possible. Doors that had been previously closed to us suddenly opened up. It was like now that we were business people, the *Americanos* no longer saw us as *Mejicanos,* but instead as other business people. It was like a miracle, I tell you, so you now go and see these nuns and priests and do not be surprised that—with the help of Our Sacred Blessed Mother and Her Son Jesus—that this might end up . . . not just being the most important talk of your life, but also a whole new miraculous change of life for you here in your heart, *con el favor de Dios,*" she added, making the sign of the cross and then kissing the back of her right thumb which she'd placed over her index finger, making a cross.

"Oh, *mama,*" I said.

"Eh, don't you 'oh, mama' me," she said. "You pray tonight, *mijito,* you pray and ask Our Lord Jesus to teach you how to find it in your heart to forgive just as He did on the cross and how your father was also able to do with Hoskins. And I'm not saying that this is easy, *mijito,* because only now that I'm approaching my last few years am I finally beginning to understand what forgiveness is really all about."

"And what's that, mama?"

"Forgiveness, *mijito,*" she said, "I'm now beginning to see is . . . is the only way for we mortals can find peace in our hearts." She stopped and took in a big breath. "So I can now see that your father . . . was absolutely right that day he went to see that no good doctor, but I just couldn't see it back then, and . . . and, well, sometimes I still have trouble seeing it even today."

It was me who now took in a big, deep breath and blew out fast. This was a big one for my mother. Maybe even the biggest. Yes, my mother was showing a lot of guts to admit this.

"Me, too, *mama*," I now said, "me, too. Oh, that little nun! Do you realize that every woman I've ever been attracted to since then has had some kind of likeness to my little nun? AND THEY DESTROYED HER, *MAMA!*" I yelled. "THEY REALLY DID!"

But my mother didn't panic or get flustered by my outburst and simply said, "Well, then, *mijito,* maybe this is exactly what you're supposed to speak about to these old nuns and priests. Remember, they, too, were young once and . . . and maybe they, too, were destroyed, and this is why they got mean."

I nodded, and nodded again. Maybe what my mother was saying was right. After all, all through my writing I always wrote—like Anne Frank had so well written in her diary—that no matter what, she still believed that people were basically good of heart.

"Okay, *mama,*" I said. "I'll pray, I really will, and I'll ask for guidance, and then I'll go see them. Thank you. You've really been a big help. Thank you very much."

"I'm glad I was able to help you, *mijito,* because . . . as you well know . . . I've never been a very good talker like your father and his mother. Oh, how that little skinny Indian woman could talk. I swear, the birds would come out of the sky to hear her speak," she added with laughter.

And so we hugged in a big *abrazo,* and then I went back across the grass and the chicken coops to the big old house that was so rundown that my parents had been very smart to want to move into the nice new smaller house. I could hear the goats and the horses in the distance and, of course, the chickens when I went inside to collect the eggs. I was feeling pretty good now. I was no longer all-divided and confused inside. No, I was now centered, and the teaching of my Native American *mamagrandes*—through *mi mama*—had done it once again. After all, when it was all said and done, we, Human People, really were like the weeds, as my dad had always said, indestructible as we reached for the Light of God!

# Two

Oh, I'd always loved flying!

In high school my best friend, John Folting, got his pilot's license when he was 16 years old and he immediately took me up in a little propeller powered plane that had no doors and flew so slowly that the cars below us would go past us. We flew just a few hundred feet above the earth, and the land below us became alive with jackrabbits in the valleys, quail in the canyons, and deer on the mesas. Oh, seeing the world from a bird's point of view was spectacular and totally all new to me. Then I'll never forget, up ahead I saw that we were approaching some green meadows and little ponds and this was when I saw a waterfall that I'd never known even existed in San Diego County, but John then banked the little plane and we headed back.

"NO!" I shouted over the noise of the propellers. "Let's keep going! I want to see that waterfall and those meadows and little ponds!"

"WE CAN'T!" he yelled back at me. "That's Mexico! We can't cross international borders without advance notice and approval!"

"What border?" I shouted. "I don't see any border! That's the same kind of brush and oak trees and rocky hills as we've got here all around us!"

I'll never forget, John started laughing and laughing. "What did you expect to see, a concrete wall like they have in China?"

"Well, no," I said, feeling all embarrassed, "but I guess I did expect to at least see something."

That day I was totally shocked to find out that . . . that in reality the world was borderless, and so incredibly beautiful and full of natural abundance, and now here I was aboard a huge commercial jet and once again looking out my window as we flew across the western United States. And once more I could see that our whole Mother Earth was so fantastic and beautiful and full of abundance as I flew northeast from San Diego, California to the city of Minneapolis at the border of Minnesota and Wisconsin. And yet I could still not see any visual borders. No, everything just worked together in unity and color. First came the rocky brush covered hills of Southern California that looked like they were covered with fur and a few trees in the canyons, then came the huge valleys of agriculture with those great big green circles—so easy to irrigate because it only took one huge turning sprinkler on monstrous wheels per circle—and then there were also long straight rows of orchards stretching out for miles, and then all of this was surrounded by vast deserts painted in colors of orange and red and white with veins of blue.

Then when I thought I couldn't take in another ounce of beauty, here came the sculptured Grand Canyon with all its wonder and majesty, then, of course, next came the tall snow-capped Rocky Mountains. Oh, I was once more in love, taking in Beauty with a capital 'B' as my *mamagrande* had always taught me how to do. In fact, I'd forgotten that I was going to see old retired nuns and priests until we landed, and then it all came rushing back into me. And even though I'd prayed and asked for guidance as my mother had suggested, I still had no real idea why I'd really accepted this speaking engagement.

At the airport a man dressed in a dark suit had a sign with my name on it. I hadn't expected this. Usually when I spoke at high schools and universities, I was picked up by the teachers or professors. This was really pretty extravagant. These old nuns and priests were really putting on a show for me. The man immediately took my luggage and took me out to a long black car, put my bag in the trunk, and then quickly opened the back door of the limousine for me. I almost laughed. This really wasn't my style.

"And in a little cooler you'll find water and beer and wine and some snacks that were prepared for you," he said. "You see, we'll be taking a two hour drive from the city of Minneapolis out into the country."

"Thank you," I said, and I slipped off my small day backpack and got into the back of the big luxurious car.

Normally I liked to sit up front with the driver and visit when I came to a new place, but this time I didn't want to talk to anyone. No, I had to gather myself. My mother's words had truly gotten deep inside of me. If she was right and this was going to maybe end up being the most important talk of my life, then I still had some heavy soul searching to do.

I took in a deep breath. Ever since I'd had my talk with my mother, it also seemed like I just couldn't get Sister Theresa out of my mind. Yes, I'd only been an eight year old, and yet I'd never quit loving that kind, soft spoken little nun. How could I? Something deep inside of me had known, within the first moment I met her, that she'd been meant to be the love of my life.

Breathing deeply, I looked out the window of the big dark car as we drove away from the airport. I could see that there was a little snow on the ground and most of the trees had lost their leaves. Then we were out of the city and traveling across farm land with large barns, then we were travelling alongside a huge lake, and I could see that all this terrain was mostly flat and wooded, a very different type of terrain than the dry, rugged, wide-open western United States that I was used to. But still I also found it to be just as breathtakingly beautiful as the land that we'd flown over.

Oh, looking out at the huge lake with its tiny splashing waves, I wished that I'd really come to go fishing so I could get to know the local people and we could talk about what kind of fish they caught and what did they do to keep their lake so clean and beautiful. A large part of me still wished that . . . that I really hadn't come to see some old retired nuns and priests.

I mean, yeah, sure, my mother had explained to me that forgiveness was our only hope, and I agreed with her, but also I had to admit that forgiveness had never been my style. After all, I wasn't my brother Joseph who'd always been so kind and gentle. I was Cain. Not Abel. In fact, at my first public talk back in 1973 when my first book *MACHO!* had come out, and the keynote speaker, a famous author, was too drunk to do the keynote, so it ended up that I spoke to the 500 teachers of English in Long Beach, California, and believe me, I'd shown no forgiveness.

Sure, I'd had notes, and I'd been prepared to give a nice little talk about all the research and interviewing that

I'd had to do to write *MACHO!* but then when I'd looked out at that sea of white teachers' faces and I hadn't seen one Black, Asian, or Mexican face, my heart EXPLODED and I'd tossed my notes away, pulled down my Stetson, and I'd gone for the jugular.

"I understand you're all English teachers," I'd said with a huge booming voice.

They'd laughed, thinking that this was a compliment.

"Well," I'd continued, "I'd like you all to know that I once had an English teacher, and . . . and I hope that that English teacher dies a painful death that lasts at least a week! BECAUSE!" I'd screamed, "I can forgive bad parents because maybe it was an accident, and they didn't even want to be parents, BUT ENGLISH TEACHERS ARE NO ACCIDENT!" I'd yelled. "You guys study to become teachers! You study for years, and so no, I will not forgive you English teachers who are abusive and torture kids with commas and periods and misspelling, making them feel like less than human, because they can't seem to be able to GET IT RIGHT!"

My publisher's representative, a woman from back east who was standing to the right of me behind the stage curtains, went bonkers and came rushing towards me to get me off the stage. But I'd turned and yelled at her, too.

"GET BACK AWAY FROM ME! I will not be silenced! These teachers came to hear a writer speak, AND THEY WILL NOW HEAR A WRITER SPEAK!"

And with that conviction, I continued with my foot to the pedal, and told the 500 English teachers that, on the other hand, I prayed to God with all my heart and soul for teachers who were patient, attentive, considerate, and kind, that these would go to Heaven when they passed and they'd be rewarded with apple pie and vanilla ice cream for all of eternity.

Tears had started pouring down my face and my publisher's representative began shitting square bricks, but then to her shock, when at the end of my talk I received a standing ovation that lasted for several minutes, she quickly changed her position, acting like the whole thing had been her idea. And my book *Macho!* became a west coast bestseller, and it was reviewed by the L.A. Times and compared to the best of John Steinbeck.

So, well, then, maybe, my mother was wrong and it wasn't about forgiveness and I should just go straight for the jugular with these nuns and priests, too. I mean, that time back in 1973, I'd just gone for it with all my heart and soul and so maybe I should do the same thing again.

Hell, this was also how I'd become a writer.

I'd just gone for it with all my heart and soul come hell or high water! The year was 1960. I was 19 years old and I'd just come back from Mexico to the U.S. three days before, and all those old horrible racist feelings that I'd had growing up with since kindergarten had come EXPLODING back up inside of me, but, well, that was also another story, so I won't go into that right now.

Anyway, these were the kind of memories that were going through my head until I got hungry and reached for the little cooler that was by my feet alongside my one day backpack, and I saw that there was a pretty pink little bag attached to the cooler. I took the pretty little bag in hand and opened it and there was a red rose inside with a note.

Instantly a smile came to my face. Who would have ever thought? I took the rose in hand and smelled of it and it smelled of Heaven, and then I read the note. It was handwritten in beautiful penmanship and simply said, "Please enjoy your drive alongside our beautiful lake, and you'll find that your pastrami sandwich has extra hot mustard just like you like it." And there was no signature. Just a little hand-drawn heart with the word "love" below it.

I was stunned.

What was this all about? And how had they found out that I liked pastrami with extra hot mustard? Then when I got a beer out of the cooler, it was a Stella, my favorite, along with Modelo and Pacifico. Had these old nuns and priests spoken with my mother or with my wife Barbara? I couldn't stop smiling as I ate my thick, delicious pastrami and drank down both beers. I was sound asleep when we drove up to the huge retirement home. Waking up, I took in several deep breaths, centering myself, and glanced around. This retirement home was a great big old beautiful mansion built on a knoll over-looking the large expanse of water that we'd been following. There were Canadian Honkers on the grass and the well-maintained grass rolled all the way down to the water's edge.

I breathed again and again.

My mother had been absolutely right, there were no accidents and I wasn't a kid anymore. I was now an adult. A published author. And so if I couldn't get past my own crap, then how could I ever expect for others to get past theirs? The buck had to stop here. My God, a rose, and then a pastrami with lots of hot mustard and a Stella, the oldest beer I knew of, started in 1366.

Yeah, sure, no doubt about it, it was me who had to change my . . . thinking, because the change we wanted for the world had to start within each of us, here deep inside of our own Hearts and Souls. Not over there with abusive nuns and priests and teachers, but right here within me, you, all of us. I got out of the car. I didn't want the driver to open the door for me. I really didn't like all that subservient crap, especially when I was dressed in old worn out Levis, cowboy boots, western hat, and a beat-up sheepskin jacket. An elderly man came out to greet me. He was smiling and in regular street clothes, but still I guessed he was a priest.

"Hello," he said, with a voice full of joy. "We're so happy you accepted our invitation." He laughed. "A few of us were getting a little worried that you might not come, because of the interviews you've done and you mentioned all those abusive things that happened to you at Catholic school. Father James," he added, sticking out his hand with a big smile.

I took his hand. "Well, you guys were right," I said. "I almost didn't come. It was my mother who talked me into coming."

"Well, then, we need to thank your mother. Lupe, correct?"

I nodded. "Yes, Lupe."

"A beautiful woman," continued Father James. "Here, let me help you with your backpack. You've had a long trip."

"No, thank you," I said. "I always like to keep my pack in my own hands at all times."

"Oh," he said, as the three of us went up the stairs. And it was one at the most deliberate "oh's" I'd ever heard.

"My God, this place is beautiful," I said once we were inside.

And I meant it. The whole backside was made up of tall magnificent windows that looked out on the rolling hill of green grass and the large expanse of water. I walked up to the windows. There were two nice big fat whitetail deer just beyond the Canadian honkers by the water's edge.

"Wow! What a gorgeous place! The deer, the honkers, the natural grass, and this huge body of water that looks like a whole entire sea! Truly, a land of plenty! Is this Lake Michigan?"

"No, it's Lake Superior."

"Really? I thought Lake Michigan was the big one."

He smiled. "All five Great Lakes are very large," he said.

"Oh, and this structure, who built it?" I asked. "The fine woodwork, the window panes, the arches, the marble floors. What great expansive architecture."

"I'm glad you appreciate it," he said with a big smile. "You see, at the turn of last century this was built as a hunting lodge by a few very rich powerful men, who liked to get together now and then, so they could make some of the major decisions for our country."

"Really? For our entire nation, eh?"

"Yes, and they had barges of material brought in from Europe and floated across the lake to this remote location so they could meet in total privacy."

I started laughing.

"What is it?" he asked.

"So those tough, greedy old conniving so-and-so's finally began to fear death, and decided to give the whole place to you guys for insurance for their souls, eh?" I said, cracking up with *carcajadas*, meaning big belly shaking laughter.

"Well," he said, "I hadn't quite thought of it like that, but you might be right. Come this way," he added. "You have time to go to your room and rest before dinner, which will be very simple, then you can get a good night's rest for tomorrow's events. I hope you don't mind, but we've invited some outside teachers and administrators to join our activities."

"No, of course not," I said. "The more, the merrier!"

"Good," he said. "After reading your books, I told them that you wouldn't be intimidated."

"Which of my books have you read?"

"*Macho, Jury*, and of course, your most fabulous book, *Rain of Gold*. But I must say, I do believe that in some ways *Jury* might just be my favorite. Did Naomi really change her vote to guilty because of cat food?"

*Jury* was the true story of the minute by minute deliberations of the Juan Corona murder trial, the largest mass murder ever committed in the United States at that time.

I laughed. "Yes, she really did, and it shocked people when Juan Corona was convicted because Hawk, the defense attorney, had torn the prosecution case apart."

"So I read," he said, "but the foreman, Ernie Phillips, guided the jurors with such, well, honesty and simplicity that they all finally voted for guilty except for Naomi."

"Exactly," I said.

"But then Naomi's sister called her and told her she was leaving, that she was going back to her own home, and her cats were out of food. I couldn't put the book down, because this then told me that the whole course of history can be changed by the most trivial and meaningless of reasons."

"Yes, but also the right decision was made by the jurors," I said, taking in a deep breath, "because after the trial . . . well, Juan Corona's priest came to me and he talked, but, of course, I can never write about what he told me."

"Really?"

"Yes."

"Oh, if I'm guessing correctly it must've been haunting his soul," said Father James, also taking in a deep breath.

"Amen," I said. "Truly, I learned a lot by doing *Macho* and *Jury*. In fact, I'm sure I could have never done *Rain* if I hadn't done those two books first."

"I can now understand that very well," he said. "*Rain of Gold* is an incredible work," he added.

"Really, you think so?" I said.

"Absolutely," he said, "I've read it three times already, and I've never done that with any other book, except, of course, for the Bible."

Hearing this, I took in a deep breath. Maybe these nuns and priests had really opened up, and so maybe, just maybe, they weren't going to panic if I told them what I really thought about the Roman Catholic Church.

"Well, I'm very glad to hear this," I said to Father James, "because, you see, I quit on *Rain of Gold* many times. I'd just get all full of doubt, and the years would pass, but then I'd re-interview my parents and give it another try. I swear, the truth is that I didn't have the talent or brains with which to pull *Rain* off, and yet, each time I'd go back to it, it was like I now had, well, new insights and . . . and a deeper understanding what it was that my parents were really telling me." I laughed. "Both my dad and mom got so frustrated with me a few times that they told me I'd just become so *gringo*-ized that I was constipated in the brain and so I could never understand the world that my two Native American *mamagrandes* had come from, but I just kept trying and trying."

"Well, we're all very glad you did," he said, "because the book shows that it was inspired by God."

"Really? You think the book shows that? I mean, it took me 16 years to write *Rain* and by the time I turned it in to my New York publisher, Marc Jaffe, and all the other people I'd known at Bantam-Random House were no longer there, or had died."

"Well, I can tell you that we've all read *Rain of Gold* and we're very happy you didn't quit and completed the book," he said. "But I also I believe that we should save the rest of this conversation for the others. So now please let me just take you to your room."

"Sure, of course." I said.

And as we walked further into the grand great-looking old place, I didn't see any people anywhere. The whole place seemed deserted.

"Where is everyone?" I asked.

"At chapel, or in their rooms."

"Oh," I said, and it was now my turn to give a very deliberate 'oh.' I'd been so caught up in the grandeur of the place and talking about *Rain* that I'd almost forgotten to whom it was that I'd be speaking.

My room was on the second story and was large and beautiful with a balcony overlooking the lake. There were now four deer on the grassy area by the water's edge and another big bunch of honkers had flown in. There were now about 200 birds. I'd never been in a natural setting of such beauty and abundance. It reminded me a lot of Yosemite, California, and the famous world class Ahwanee Lodge.

I unpacked, then decided to lie down to rest for a few minutes. It was a good comfortable bed. Firm but not too firm. And I guess that, well, I fell into a deep sleep, because the next thing I knew, I awoke and it was dark and yet there was some light coming from the far end of my room. I got up on my elbows and saw that a man was standing across the room from me and a bright and yet soft golden light surrounded him.

I rubbed my eyes, thinking that I was still asleep and dreaming all this, but then I realized I was awake and breathing fast, and the man was now gone. And for the life of me, I couldn't remember where I was. So I lay back down and, little by little, I began to remember that I was at a retirement home of old nuns and priests by Lake Superior and not Lake Michigan. And that the last time I'd had a man come to me surrounded by a bright and yet soft golden light had been in Madrid, Spain and . . . and that man had been Our Lord Jesus Christ.

I sat up, took in a deep breath, and blew out fast. And back then in Spain, when Jesus had come to me, made total sense, because I'd been completely Open of Heart and . . . and my *familia* and I and a group of Native Americans had gone to Spain in the name of worldwide harmony and peace and abundance for all, and so what was I now being told by Jesus? Was I now being told that forgiveness wasn't enough, but that I also had to have a completely Open Heart*Corazon* for these nuns and priests?

Oh, my God! I got up and went to the restroom, took a long pee, then washed my hands and face. At times like this I sometimes felt like I was crazy*loco*. Who did I think I was to really think that Jesus had come to in Spain and then here in Wisconsin once again? But then, as I continued washing my face with cold water and my *mamagrandes'* teaching began coming back to me and I once more realized that there really was no separation between us and the Spirit World once we let go and we started seeing with our HeartEyes and not just our HeadEyes, then yes, of course, Jesus had just come to me now as He'd come to me in Spain and . . . and as He'd come to me the first time just north of Buccaneer Beach in South Oceanside when I'd been eight years old.

I smiled, remembering that beautiful day when I'd been eight years old.

Joseph, my brother and best friend, had just passed over a few days before, and I'd suddenly been awakened right before daybreak and told in no uncertain terms that I was supposed to go to the corrals and saddle up my brother's horse Midnight Duke.

I got up, slipped on my Levis and boots, and quickly went out to the corrals and Duke came walking up to me out of the dark as if he, too, had been told what we were supposed to do. And that day a miracle happened of horses and dolphins with my brother Joseph walking on water alongside Our Lord Jesus just beyond a big black rock and the breakers. And this was when I came to the understanding that when one of our loved ones passed over, we weren't losing them, but instead gaining an even closer relationship with Our Lord Jesus. I'll never forget, I'd been eight years old and riding a horse out in the surf surrounded by dolphins and the Father Sun had just been coming up illuminating the whole world!

And now remembering all this so vividly, brought a smile to my face and I looked in the mirror above the sink, and instantly I caught a quick flash of Jesus being behind me, and He, too, was smiling.

"Hi," I said into the mirror.

"Hello," He said from the mirror.

"Thanks for coming with me," I said.

And saying this, I began laughing and laughing with big *carcajadas.* What a ridiculous thing to say, there were no boundaries of Space and Time for Jesus, and once we accepted Him, then, of course, there were no boundaries of Space and Time for us, and so He was always with us. It wasn't like He would have stayed behind in California and I'd come to Wisconsin by myself. And He now started laughing and laughing, too, and it felt so good. Yeah, sure, of course, it wasn't bad for me to be crazy*loco.* Hell—I mean Heaven—there was really no other way to live, except being crazy*loco* full of Love*Amor!* After all, Life, *la Vida,* was a VoyageDream and Confucius had said it best:

> Row, row, row your boat,
> Gently down the stream,
> Merrily, merrily, merrily,
> Life is but a dream!

Oh, I was suddenly feeling so happy! BIG BIG HAPPY! Feeling the Presence of Jesus always felt so good, I just couldn't stop smiling. I slipped on my Levis, and went across the room to the balcony to look up at the stars. But opening the balcony door, the freezing cold hit me like a wall of ice. I quickly closed the door.

Shivering, I went across the room and got back in bed under the big warm comforter. And as I lay in bed, I began to realize that Jesus was always really, really, really with me, with you, with all of us when we were Open of Heart like I'd been in Spain and He'd come to endorse our movement of Snow Goose Global Thanksgiving, meaning that we were taking our greatest U.S. celebration of

Thanksgiving, when Native Americans and Europeans ate in harmony and peace together, and going global with it. And so Jesus had now come to me again, because He was endorsing this talk I was going to have with these old retired nuns and priests.

Tears came to my eyes. Yes, of course, this was it, but I just hadn't seen it, because once more I was such a Doubting Thomas. OH, WHEN WAS I EVER GOING TO LEARN?!?

I breathed.

I breathed again and again and I guess that I went back to sleep, because the next thing I knew, I awoke and there was sunlight coming in my window. Why, I'd slept the whole night through. The whole eastern sky was now painted in gorgeous colors of red and orange and pink with spectacular streaks of dazzling blue and soft purple. I took in several deep breaths, blew out fast, got up, found I was still wearing my Levis, and crossed the room to step out on the balcony, and to my surprise, the cold didn't hit me like a wall of ice this time. No, it was like the cold now embraced me with a crisp, good feeling of energizing Love*Amor*.

I laughed.

I smiled. It felt so invigorating that I quickly put both of my hands over my heart, and began giving greetings to the Father Sun as I'd been doing ever since I began to write on the 16th of September 1960 at 6 a.m. back home on the *rancho* in South Oceanside at the north end of Stewart Street.

"GOOD MORNING! GOOD MORNING! GOOD MORNING, FATHER SUN!" I shouted, pounding my heart area with both of my open hands and looking out at the Sun, the Right Eye of God.

"FROM MY HEART!" I shouted again, pounding again. "Good morning Father Sun! Goodnight Mother Moon," who was, of course, the Left Eye of God. "*Con todo mi corazon*, good morning, good morning, Father Sky, Mother Earth, and All Our Holy Stars, *nuestra familia!* Our great great grandparents and aunts and uncles! All of Our Ancestry who've already come here to *Tierra Santa* and completed their Holy Work for the Almighty and His/Her ongoing Sacred Garden of Heaven on Mother Earth!

"FROM MY HEART, GOOD MORNING! GOOD MORNING!" I shouted even louder, giving Love*Amor* with all my Heart and Soul to the whole entire Universe! "Good morning, *familia!* Good morning! Good morning! GOOD MORNING!"

And I now began laughing with *carcajadas!*

Oh, it felt so good down deep inside to be doing this Sacred Holy Ritual of giving thanks that my *mamagrande* had taught to do when I'd been a child and I'd been performing every single day since then, giving thanks to the Almighty for His/Her precious gift of *otro milagro!*

I breathed and breathed and glanced around and saw that the honkers were already up and munching, like an army of great big birds, bobbing their heads up and down in a quick singing rhythm as they ate the tips off the grass. And the lake waters were shimmering and splashing and the trees were also singing in the breeze. Oh, it was a symphony of life and sound and color, and then two white tail deer suddenly came prancing by with their ears pointing forward and highly alert.

Something must've startled them, and then I saw them, Five Native Americans, dressed in buckskin and fur, and they were walking about three feet above the ground just like Jesus had hovered about two feet above the floor when He'd come to me this morning and when He'd come to me in Spain. I called out, waving to my Five Native Brothers, and they turned and waved back to me, then they, too, ShapeShifted out of this Dimension and into another just as Jesus had also done so easily.

# Three

So I went back inside, did my floor exercises, showered, dressed, and went down for breakfast. I was starving. In the lobby, I saw people going to a room to the right just off of the huge, beautiful main dining room. I followed them, thinking they might lead me to food. There were about 30 people in the smaller room. They were all elderly and dressed in street clothes and most of them were women. The men, who were very few, were all over by the food which was set out on two long white linen covered tables by the large expanse of windows overlooking the grass and the lake.

I could now see that it had been a good thing that I'd slept through the whole night and I hadn't met any of these people for dinner last night, because, well, I'm sure that if I'd met them last night, I would have probably just been looking at them and trying to figure out which nun had been the meanest and which priest had been the child molester. But now that I'd slept the whole night through and Jesus had come to me as He'd done in Madrid, Spain, I was seeing things very differently. Simply, I was seeing these nuns and priests as just happy looking old people.

Father James was the first one to come up to me. "Good morning," he said with a great big smile. "How did you sleep?"

"Very well, thank you," I said. "How about you? How did you sleep?"

"Not so good. It's hard to sleep at my age."

"Oh, how old are you?"

"I'm going on 82," he said.

"My dad was older than you and every night he slept like a baby," I said.

"Well, I wish I knew his secret," he said, laughing. "In fact, I bet many of us would like to know."

And I almost said, "Well, maybe my dad slept like a baby because he had a clear conscious and a lot of you guys don't." But I didn't say this, and instead just kept quiet. After all, I had to keep an Open Heart as Jesus had let me know, especially if I hoped to accomplish anything worthwhile with all these old nuns and priests.

"I'll be introducing you," he continued. "Is there anything special that you'd like me to say?"

"No, not really. Just go for it, but please keep it short, okay?"

"Of course," he said.

Then he walked me over to the two tables where the food was laid out.

"As you can see," he said, "we mostly have rolls and coffee and fruit, but there are also eggs and bacon available. You never came down for dinner last night, did you?" he added.

"No, I didn't," I said, "and I'm starving, so yes, I'd really like to have a big full breakfast." I laughed. "I had such vivid wonderful dreams I awoke laughing!"

"Really? You awoke laughing?"

"Yes, and it was wonderful!"

"I'll be," he said. "Maybe it's hereditary. Your grand-mother, *Doña Margarita*—I hope I pronounced it right—if I'm not mistaken, awoke laughing many times, too."

"Yes, you pronounced very well, and you're right. My grandmother would explain to us that when we sleep, our Guardian Angel takes us back up to Heaven to sleep in the Holy Arms of *Papito Dios*, so how can we not awake laughing, eh?"

"Well, maybe this is something you can tell us all about, too," he said. "You see, this is what many of us found so fascinating about your book. It was almost like your grandmothers didn't worship God, but instead—how can I say this—they lived with God."

"Exactly, because in many native languagings, breath-ing and God are the exact same word."

"Really? Oh, you will definitely need to tell us about this!"

"I'll be glad to," I said.

Wow, I was really beginning to see that it was a Godsend that I'd come. What a waste it had been for me to carry around inside of me all this hate and rage for nuns and priests all these years. But, well, on the other hand, maybe it hadn't been a waste, because my rage and hate had also been part of my main driving force through all those years of rejection.

Father James had them prepare two eggs and four crisp pieces of bacon for me and also a mountain of country potatoes, and a couple of slices of rye toast with butter and strawberry jam on the side. I ate everything and drank down two full cups of my own Yogi herbal tea that I always carried with me in my backpack, and now I was ready.

Most people had taken their seats, and I could see that almost everyone had a copy of *Rain of Gold,* and a few also had *Macho!* and *Jury.* My next two books, that would complete the trilogy of *Rain of Gold, Thirteen senses* and *Wild Steps of Heaven,* wouldn't be out for another year.

Father James and a very handsome young-looking man were making a final check of the microphone. I took in a deep breath and walked across the room in my western boots over towards the podium that was by the large expanse of windows. Glancing out, I saw that the whitetail deer were gone, but most of the Canadian honkers were still grazing on the grass outside the huge windows. Other honkers were lying down and resting. I smiled. Oh, I just loved this beautiful natural setting!

Then Father James called people to order and did my introduction, but he didn't keep it short like he'd agreed to do. Instead he did like a lot of teachers and professors did and he praised my work, my talent, and especially my tenacity of having endured over 265 rejections from New York publishers. And then he still didn't stop and he went on to say how my first book *Macho!* was immediately compared to the best of John Steinbeck by the *Los Angeles Times.* This always embarrassed me to no end, because, in my opinion, John Steinbeck—and not Hemingway or Fitzgerald—had to be the best writer of our country, truly giving voice to the real people of our nation. And then to further embarrass me, he added that it was an honor I'd come to be with them.

"In fact, he almost didn't accept our invitation until his mother Lupe convinced him to come," he added with laughter.

After receiving some applause and cheering, I walked over to Father James and gave him a big hug, and at first he resisted, but then relaxed and hugged me back. I thanked him and stepped up to the podium as he walked over and took a seat along with the priests who were all in the back.

"Thank you," I said. "Thank you very much, and the honor is really mine to be here. And I loved that red rose and the note and that thick wonderful pastrami with lots of extra hot mustard that you guys put in the little cooler for me in the limo."

The faces of the nuns directly in front of me lit up with joy. I smiled and nodded to them, and they all smiled and nodded back, except for one cute little short nun with grey curly hair who turned all red with embarrassment, and quickly glanced away. Oh, then this maybe meant that the others didn't know about the flower and the note.

I laughed and glanced around. All the nuns were in the first three rows, and the priests were all behind them, and some of these hadn't even taken their seats yet. I closed my eyes. I wasn't going to let this bother me, so I just took in a deep breath, gathering myself deep inside, then . . . then I realized that I had absolutely no idea where to begin. I'd never spoken to a roomful of nuns and priests before. I usually spoke to teachers, professors, students, law enforcement groups, and/or other community organizations.

I kept my eyes closed and asked for guidance, and it came to me to start out with a story, and maybe even the story of my nephew Erik and how I'd taken him to the beach that day, but then . . . no, no. I thought this might be too strong, especially if I concluded about the incoming and outgoing waves being like our Mother Earth's 26,000 year cycle of male and female global energy.

Then out of the blue it came to me to start with a science-driven story that I'd never used before in order to help get them out of the limited world of their well-educated heads. Then after I accomplished this, I could then ask them to please join me in a Native American prayer that I'd learned a few years back, and by doing these two things, then I'd have a better feel of where I could go with these nuns and priests without losing them.

"GOOD MORNING!" I said in a loud voice. "Good morning! Good morning! Good morning! How did you all sleep? Good, I hope. Myself, I slept like a baby and awoke smiling and laughing, then I when out on my balcony and I saw the Father Sun, the Right Eye of God, coming up with all His splendor and wonder, which, according to my two Indian *mamagrandes* makes every day *otro milagro de Dios*, another Miracle straight from God, as you already know since . . . since you've read *Rain of Gold.*"

I stopped. My heart was pounding. Something was happening to me deep inside. I just couldn't start out with a little story. No, first I'd have to bluntly tell them why it was that I almost hadn't accepted this speaking engagement.

"But now," I said, "before I can begin my talk or . . . or even ask you to share with me why you invited me to come to see you, I first need to let all of you know that Father James was right, and I almost didn't accept this speaking engagement, because . . . because of all the abuse I received at the hands of nuns and priests as a young boy."

Tears came to my eyes and I took in several deep breaths and I could well see that I'd definitely surprised them and a few even looked like they were ready to bolt.

"But please bear with me," I said, closing my eyes, "because, you see, it's going to, well, turn out for the good." I opened my eyes and blew out fast. "After days of procrastination, I went to see my mother and we had a *quesadilla* with homemade *salsa* and avocado, and she, who you all know as Lupe in the book and is now almost 90 years old, told me in no uncertain terms that I had to find forgiveness in my heart just as Our Lord Jesus had done on the cross, and come and see all of you because this could very well end up being the most important talk of my life."

The tears were now running down my face. "Look, I was eight years old when I fell in love with the little young nun who was teaching me how to read after school in the fourth grade." I wiped the tears off my face. "She was so kind to me. In fact, she was my first teacher who didn't make me feel stupid because I didn't get it. You see, I'm dyslexic and didn't learn to read until I was 20, and it's a miracle that I was ever able to become a writer."

"Would you like some water?" asked the little short nun with the curly grey hair.

"Yes," I said. "Please."

She quickly got up and went to the two large tables where the food had been laid out, poured me a glass of water from a large pitcher, and then brought the water and a handful of napkins for me.

"Thank you," I said, taking the water and napkins to dry my eyes. "And you are?"

"Mary, Sister Mary, but just call me Mary," she said.

"Thank you, Mary," I said, drinking down the whole glass and then wiping my tears. "Are you the one who wrote me the note and put the rose in the little bag?"

"Yes," she said, getting slightly embarrassed, "but please just go on. We really want to know who this man is who wrote *Rain of Gold*. Most of us girls just knew that it had to be a woman."

I laughed. "Well, in a way it really was a woman," I said, "because it was my mother and my aunts and my godmother whom I interviewed, and *mi papa* had also been raised in the old Indian way as a woman by his old Indian mother for the first seven years of his life, meaning that he learned to do the work around the house and helped in the birthing process of the goats and dogs and cats, and then even of his older cousins and sisters, and such a man," I now added, "doesn't grow up thinking that women are the weaker sex, but instead is in complete awe of women, and this is one of the Eight Indigenous Concepts that will help reverse the course of modern civilization."

I could see that my mention of the Eight Native American Concepts that would take all of us Back To The Future had rattled a lot of cages, but I couldn't stop and explain now, and so I quickly went on.

"But anyway," I said, "getting back to the story of my little nun, my dad had always told me that the most important decision any man can make in his life is choosing the right woman to marry, because the woman a man married would not just be his wife but the first teacher of his children. And so after a couple of weeks of being with my little nun every day after school, I could see that she was by far the kindest, smartest, most wonderful woman I'd ever met, and so naturally I asked her if she would marry me when I grew up. But she told me that she was already married to Jesus.

"'He's dead, you know,' I'd said

"'Yes, but I'm married to Our Lord Jesus in Spirit,' she'd said.

"'Oh, then that's okay,' I'd said, 'we can get married in body and have babies.'

"And she then smiled this most beautiful smile, and looking back, I can guess that she was now going to explain to me what she meant by being married in Spirit, but she never got to say this to me, because at that very moment the big mother superior came bursting in through the door and she slapped me so hard she knocked me out of my chair, called me the devil, and then started hitting my kind, wonderful, little nun who wouldn't fight back or even try to defend herself, and so this was when I attacked the old nun, biting her leg so hard that she quit hitting my little nun.".

I stopped. My heart was pounding. And I could see that I'd startled half of the nuns, and others were in tears, but the priests, a few of them looked like they now wanted to hit me, too.

"But now let's not stop here," I said, heart still pounding, "because I'd like to bring that incident that happened 40-some years ago to the present and ask how many of you had experiences with a little kid like this? And you don't have to raise your hands. No, what I really want for you to do is just go within yourself, to your own Kingdom of God, and see if you ever behaved like this mother superior or the little nun, because that wasn't the end of that situation.

"Oh, no, after that, the young priest, who was attached to the school and the old mother superior, thought it was their duty to keep beating me on a weekly schedule and tell me that I'd been born with Original Sin and so they were punishing me for my own good, so I wouldn't go to hell and burn for eternity."

I wiped the tears out of my eyes. "But now looking back, what I think was really going on was that both, that young priest and the old mother superior, were in love with my beautiful young nun and they were jealous that they'd never proposed marriage to her."

I glanced around. "And I'm not joking," I added. "Recently, I've had the good fortune to become friends with some ex-nuns and ex-sisters of different religious organizations, and they've told me that part of the reason they left their organizations was because of the sexual advances that had been made on them by their superiors, both male and female."

I stopped, taking in a deep breath. "And I'm not blaming or finger pointing. I'm just saying that there are no accidents in life, and that we are a very emotional and sexually driven planet, and so we need to understand this and admit it, so that then everyday can, indeed, become *otro milagro de Dios,* instead of a living hell, because of all of our hypocrisy, and hidden agendas and lies.

"And so yes, I'm glad that I came to see you guys, because the buck needs to stop here, right now, so together we can do some serious healing, and . . . and not just of the body and mind, but also of our Hearts and Souls." I breathed and then added, "And so thank you, thank all of you here very much for having invited me to come to see you, for you and I now have a great—" Two priests had gotten to their feet. "No, please, don't leave!" I said. "This is good! This is wonderful!"

"Yes, he's right, you know," said a tall elegant nun who was sitting beside little Sister Mary. "Mother Teresa always says, "I know that God will not give me anything I can't handle, but I only wish that He didn't have so much trust in me."

Many of the nuns nodded in agreement, but I could see that quite a few of the priests looked like they were ready to bolt, and not just these two who'd stood up. I closed my eyes, asked for guidance, then decided to take the bull by the horns.

"Look," I said to the two priests, "leave if you must, but also realize that this will only cause people to think the worst of you." I opened my eyes. "And so I suggest that you two stay and we all see this through together. Because, like my mother so well said to me before I left, '*Mijito,* all my life I've found that miracles often come to us when we least expected it, and when we're doing exactly what it is that we've been avoiding and not wanting to do.' And then my mother told me to open up my heart and pray and realize that there are no accidents, only situations that can cause us to Spiritually grow beyond our wildest dreams. So please, stay and let us dream together."

"Yes," spoke the tall, elegant-looking nun again, "and this was exactly what Teresa was talking about and . . . and what is now causing me to have to consider if I ever behaved like that mother superior when I was in that position."

"Thank you," I said to this ex-mother superior, "this is truly wonderful, and so now what I'm proposing is that we all fasten our seatbelts because . . . because we're now going into the Kingdom of God that's within each of us, and hence OUT, OUT, OUT TO THE FURTHEST STARS, and into a reality beyond our five-sensory perception and into OUR NATURAL MULTI-SENSORY PERCEPTION OF 13 SENSES, AND INFINITE POSSIBILITIES!

"And this is no joke! But the very foundation of *Rain of Gold,* which means a rain of Miracles coming down to us from God on a daily basis! You see, most people miss the point and simply read *Rain* as a history book about two families and the Mexican Revolution, and then coming to the United States, but this isn't what *Rain of Gold* is really all about. It's about—"

"Faith in God!" said Sister Mary. "And about learning to see nature in a way that I'd never read about in any other book, and then your mother Lupe, a seven-year-old child, waking up every day to the first three miracles of the day."

"It's about a family, who in their innocence, still lives in the Garden of Eden, saying that every woman needs her own crying tree, and then butterflies coming into their box canyon in a dancing cloud of dazzling golden color and land among all the beautiful wild orchids and other gorgeous flowers!" said another nun.

"It's about the love of a seven-year-old girl for her knight in shining armor, and how she has to make tough decisions that would intimidate even grown women."

"It's about forgiveness and gratitude and going on, no matter what."

"It's about seeing every day as another Miracle given to us by God."

"It's about life and a kind loving God, and never getting bitter, even after witnessing your children being raped and killed before your very eyes."

"Yes," said Sister Mary, turning to the nun who'd spoken last, "but it doesn't stop there. Even after *Dona Margarita,* my favorite character, looses 11 of her 14 children, she still goes to her outhouse, smokes her little *cigarillo,* drinks her coffee laced with *whiskito,* and she says her rosary. Oh, to have such relaxed, natural Faith no matter what, this is what *Rain of Gold* is really all about!"

I pulled up a chair and sat down and my eyes filled with tears of joy. These nuns had really read *Rain of Gold* and they'd really, really gotten it, but the priests, as a group, still didn't join them.

"Oh, my God, thank you, thank you, thank you!" I said, getting up, after half of the nuns had spoken. "And I almost didn't come. Oh, what a Doubting Thomas I am! But truly, I can now see that we're going to have a fine time, because I can now see that a lot of you here are ready to receive beyond your wildest dreams! You see, myself, I've been receiving beyond my wildest dreams ever since I took an oath before God up in the wilds of Wyoming to become not just a writer, but a writer as great as Homer and/or greater with the help of Our Lord God."

"How old were you?" asked a priest.

"Oh, nineteen, or maybe a week into being 20. I'd just gotten back from Mexico where I'd found my roots just as Alex Haley had found his in Africa."

"You were only 19 when you took that oath?" asked this same priest.

"Well, why not? Didn't most of you here take a similar oath at 18, 19, or 20 to dedicate your lives to the service of God? So that's what I did, too. But I can tell you that it wasn't until my dad passed over and I was in my late 40s that my Spiritual Education EXPLODED INTO MIRACLES! And I then came to the full realization that I'd been receiving from the University of the Divine ever since I'd taken my oath. And you guys have also been receiving from this same Divine University whether you realize it or not.

"And this evening after dinner," I continued, "I'll be able to guide you on how to receive in your sleep, just as my dad explained to me on the night before he passed over. And then tomorrow morning I'll ask you about your dreams, and you'll see how, as a group, as a Collective Consciousness of Dreaming, you people will start leading, and I'll be the one who'll start following in front!"

"Following in front?" asked a priest.

"Yes, that's what the big male goose does when he's at the head of a V-formation of geese, cutting the wind so that all the rest of the geese can then use 30% less energy to keep up. But no more about this right now. Right now I need for all of you to fasten your seatbelts, because . . . because we first need to gain the understanding of the Eight Western Civilization Concepts that are holding us back from worldwide Harmony and Peace and Abundance for All, and once we grasp these eight concepts, we will then be able to slipslide back into the Indigenous Concepts that will free us, then BOOM! We explode into Our Natural All-Knowing Cellular Memory, and each of you will then start remembering that we come from the Stars, Our True Home, and you'll also Know deep inside of yourself all about Our Six Sister Planets that Our Mother Earth belongs to.

"You see, all of you already Know all this deep inside your Collective Cellular Memory, and this is why Jesus so well said that what He did, we, Collectively, would do more, and in doing more, we will automatically Harmonize into World Wide Peace and Abundance for All, because this is a natural part of our DNA, and all of our Six Sister Planets have already realized this eons of timeless time ago!"

The same two priests leaped to their feet.

"Oh, please," I said, closing my eyes, "just sit your asses back down! Didn't Jesus say that we all have the Kingdom of God within us? Well, then, the Kingdom of God must include everything there is, and so I'm not really saying anything new! Come on, guys, just sit back down, and I promise you that all this will start making sense in just a little bit.

"You see," I said, opening my eyes, "*Rain of Gold* is just the first book of a trilogy, so what you people have read is just the tip of the iceberg. Remember, Hemingway said that the dignity of the movement of an iceberg is that 7/8 is under water, and so we're just getting started, guys."

Hearing this, both old priests sat back down.

"Thank you," I said, "thank you very much. You see, I didn't come here with loaded guns. I really did as my mother told me to do and I asked for guidance, and when I went to bed that night I understood that yes, I was supposed to come out here and see you, and then last night, right here, in my room upstairs, *mi papa*, who'd passed over 10 years ago, came to me in my sleep and he assured me that my mother was right, and that it was pre-ordained that all of us come together. So come on, let's just go for it! Okay?" The two priests nodded. "Good. Thank you. And so now I'm going to first start with a little story, and then I'm going to ask you all to join me in a Native American prayer that will set up what this whole talk will really be all about. Okay, ready?"

Once again, all the nuns nodded, but quit a few of the priests still looked pretty guarded.

"Okay, not long ago I read an article about two young *Latino* astronomers," I said, "and the article explained how these two young guys had come to the conclusion that all the telescopes around the world had grey-green lenses, and that grey-green wasn't part of the natural colors of a rainbow. So these two guys then speculated that if the rainbow color of rose was put on the huge telescope in Baja, California, where the sky is still relatively clean and there are no city lights for 100s of miles, then these new stars that had recently been found would turn out not to be stars, but entire new galaxies and galaxies, because of the higher frequency of their natural rose-colored lens.

"Well, these two young Chicano astronomers were finally able to get the funding to do it, and they found out that these new stars were, indeed, new galaxies and new galaxies, and then when they turned their rose-colored lenses to other well-established parts of the heavens, they discovered other new galaxies, too, and our comprehension of the heavens quadrupled exponentially, and they almost hadn't been allowed to do their work by the old well-established astronomers. Pretty good, eh? And so this is what I'm now proposing that we do. That we put on rose-colored glasses like in that old Frank Sinatra song, and that you please join me in this Native American prayer that I learned from my good friend Lydia Whirlwind Soldier of the Lakota Nation.

"Eh, would you please do me the honor and join me? You see, this is also what my two Indigenous *mamagrandes* always did. They'd wouldn't look at the world through the low frequency of the grey-green glasses of Western Civilization, but instead, they'd keep their vibrant rose-colored glasses on, and they'd mix their Indian Spirituality with their Catholic Christianity, and, in doing this, they'd come up with a wonderful new way of giving Daily Thanks to Our Holy Creator. All right, now everyone please stand up!"

All the nuns immediately stood up. The priests were a little slower to follow, but they all finally got to their feet, too.

"Okay, good," I said. "Thank you. And now, put your left hand, palm open, and facing up, and put your right hand, palm open, and facing down. Good. Good. Perfect."

All the nuns were participating, but even though all of the priests had stood up, only about half of them were doing what I asked. I closed my eyes. I was not going to let this bother me. I sent them all Love*Amor,* and then when I opened my eyes, a few more of the priests began participating. And I also noticed that the young, very handsome priest, who was sitting next to Father James, looked totally open and big happy.

"Okay, now, please, everyone close your eyes," I said, "and breathe in deeply, activating your Kingdom of God that Jesus so wisely told us about. Good. Good. And now imagine yourself to be a Hollow Bone. A Buffalo Bone. And with your left hand facing up and open, you are receiving, receiving, receiving good-feeling harmonious energy from our whole entire Universe! Just like Albert Einstein did when he received his great theory!" I said with a loud clear voice and with my eyes still closed. "And with your right hand open and facing down you are flooding the Mother Earth with all this good, wonderful, healthy, Pure Love Energy you are receiving even from the . . . the FURTHEST REACHES OF THE UNIVERSE!

"Breathe, breathe, and realize that the faster you give, the faster you receive, so you keep giving and giving and giving as you keep receiving and receiving and . . . and receiving, and you keep *nada, nada,* nothing for yourself, because you are a Hollow Bone, a Buffalo Bone, and you are so huge, so great that your head and hands and feet stretch out to the ends of Creation; receiving, receiving, receiving, and Our Sacred Mother Earth is no larger than a grain of sand on the Seashore of Creation, and we, Human Beings, are Holy Instruments of receiving and giving.

"And understand that old Albert knew this to his bones! That we are all Hollow Bones! Buffalo Bones once we've activated the Kingdom of God that's within each of us! And then at this point we, all of us, become the Almighty's Holy instruments of spreading His/Her Love*Amor* throughout the Universe! Because this is who we, Human Beings, really are, Holy Sacred Instruments of receiving and giving and this is why, when I was eight years old, I was able to receive the vision of seeing my brother Joseph, three days after he'd passed over, walking on the ocean just out beyond the breakers alongside Jesus."

"You saw Jesus?"

I opened my eyes. "Yes, I saw Jesus," I said.

"In full three-dimensional form?"

"Well, yes, of course, but please, just let me go on, because, you see, the time has come in our Godelution for all of us to start walking alongside Jesus right now, right here on Mother Earth."

"Godelution?" mumbled another priest, opening his eyes, too.

"Yes," I said, "Godelution is also one of the Eight Indigenous Concepts that we need in order for us to slipslide and/or dissolve ourselves back into the Holy Garden. Evolution and God do not necessary have to oppose each other."

"Makes perfect sense!" shouted a nun, who was keeping her eyes closed.

"Not to me," said a priest, opening his eyes.

And I could now see that almost everyone had their eyes open.

"Okay," I said to the priest, "I can understand why you'd say that, but now tell me, have you ever walked into a room and you instantly knew something was wrong? Come on, how many of you have had this experience?"

Almost everyone raised their hands, especially the nuns who still had their eyes closed.

"Good. Excellent. And you didn't think this," I said, "you knew this, because thinking is done with manmade words which are very recent in our development as Human Beings, and on the other hand, feelings are ancient. Maybe 100s of 1000s of years old, and/or maybe even millions of years old, and we feel not just done with our hands, but with our whole body 26 arm-lengths in all directions. And old cops immediately know what I'm talking about, because when they come to a potentially violent situation, they automatically quit their thinking and start trusting their gut-feelings, their instinct, which is the voice of our genius which processes information 10,000 times faster than thinking."

I stopped and glanced around. Only a few still had their eyes closed. "And so what I'm saying," I continued, "is that we all now need to quit our thinking, so we can get out of our Head Computer and move into our Heart Computer, and only then can we access our Soul Computer, and enter into the Kingdom of God that's within each of us.

"Truly understand that our five senses we got from the Greeks, from Aristotle, I believe, is one of the Eight

Western Concepts that is holding us back, and our Full Natural 13 Sensory Multi-Perception, that came to me from my *mamagrande* from *Oaxaca, Mexico* is what will free us, because we do, in fact, have three computers for processing information. The Head Computer with four senses, the Heart Computer with three senses, and the Soul Computer with six senses, and we'll go into all of this later on, but now please just breathe, breathe, and understand that the longest journey that any of us will ever make are those 18 inches from our head to our heart."

I stopped and breathed. "Good, good," I said. "I can now see that most of you are participating with me and breathing deeply, too. Excellent. And so now please tell me how did that Native American prayer make you feel deep inside? Pretty good, eh?

A lot of people nodded, saying yes.

"Good. I'm glad to hear this, because I'll tell you, the first time I heard this prayer, it touched me to the depths of my being. My God, for us to be the Sacred Instruments of spreading Love*Amor* for God was so beautiful! So fantastic! And made so much sense! Then we, Human Beings, really can walk on water alongside Jesus because we're part of God's Creating Light. And this, in a nutshell, is what Albert Einstein did to receive his theory and what I'll be talking about for the next two days. Okay, now the rest of you please open your eyes," I said. "And now please turn and look at each other. Do you now see yourselves differently?" I asked. "Do you see a light?"

Several nuns nodded and said that they did.

"Good," I said, "so will one of you tell us about this Light you see?"

Mary, the curly grey-haired little nun, spoke first. "When I first opened my eyes I thought I saw a Light surrounding Sister *Margarita*, but now I'm not quite sure."

"Exactly," I said, "when I first began to see a bright and yet soft golden Light around people, I thought it was just my imagination. But then I also began to see a crescent shaped little Moon just off to my right when I got up to write and I'd go to the bathroom to wash my face. Then it soon began happening to me so regularly that I knew it was really real and not just my imagination.

"So what I'm saying is that this Light that some of you saw, especially you people who kept your eyes closed the whole time so you were able to keep your focus, will now start happening to you more and more regularly, and then BOOM! You, too, will then one day see your own Crescent Moon, and soon that Moon will soon be so bright and steady that you won't have to turn on the bathroom light when you get up in the middle of the night to go to the bathroom. And . . . and most important, you'll be feeling, oh, so happy! BIG BIG HAPPY!"

"That's true," said Mary. "When I saw this Holy Light surrounding Sister *Margarita*, it was like I was receiving all this understanding, all these feelings that we're all Holy, and that I still have a lot of life to live," she said, with tears of joy coming to her eyes. "Like I now understand that my life of service is far from over, and this makes me so happy!"

"BIG, BIG HAPPY, eh?" I shouted.

"Yes! BIG BIG HAPPY!"

I laughed. She laughed.

"And all of you who were able to keep your eyes closed the whole time, are you now beginning to see that there's a whole world out here, within us, that's Alive with the Living Breath of God?"

"Is this why you continually close your eyes," asked a nun who had not spoken yet, "and take in such deep breaths?"

"Yes, exactly," I said. "And I'd like all of you to notice that when Mary spoke she never used the word 'thinking' in reference to the Light she saw. She used the words 'understanding' and then 'feelings', and this is, because thinking, which processes information through manmade words, is so superficial and limiting that we can never come to Know God with thinking. Albert Einstein wasn't thinking when he came up with his theory. No, he was flashing with Light of Divine Understanding, and this is called receiving through your Guardian Angel and/or Genuising."

"Yes," said a nun in the second row, "it was a wonderful experience for you to have us close our eyes, because with my eyes closed I wasn't distracted even with what was being said, and I actually got to feeling so strongly connected to God that, of course, I just wanted to keep giving and giving forever!"

"Exactly," I said. "You see, greed is not part of human nature. What is part of human nature is birthing God."

"Birthing God!?!" said several priests and one nun.

"Yes, this is another Indigenous Concept that we all used to understand when we remembered our Original Instruction. Why do you think that religions are so strong all over the world? We're all trying to birth God, to give Life to God from deep inside of us. Truly, greed only happens when we lose contact with God that's here within us. You all read how my grandmother *Doña Margarita* gave

away all the money that the rich man gave her in *Arandas, Jalisco* when she was on her way to save her son, Jose, the
Great, from execution."

"That's not in *Rain of Gold,*" said a couple of nuns.

"Oh, that's right," I said, laughing. "That didn't get into *Rain*. This is in *Wild Steps of Heaven*. You see, originally *Rain* was 1,500 pages, so I ended up breaking it down into three books. Anyway, my dad explained to me that when people think money will solve all of their *problemas,* then it is very difficult if not impossible for them to see or ever receive any Miracles from the Almighty.

"Truly, Collectively, understand that we all need to once more start becoming Hollow Bones, Buffalo Bones, Instruments of receiving God's Holy Light, just as Albert Einstein did when he saw himself riding on that beam of light and he came up with his Theory of Relativity. You see, this is exactly who we, Human Beings, really are once we activate Our Kingdom of God that's within each of us, we become . . . Beams of the Almighty's Holy Light, giving and giving and giving in ABUNDANCE!

"Remember, Supreme Being is one of the original terms we used for God, and we are Human Beings, and so old Einstein was right when he saw himself riding on a beam of light. No, he'd actually seen himself become a Beam of Holy Light, and this is who all of us really, really are. And I, myself, I could never really grasp this until I first learned to see myself as a Hollow Bone, a Buffalo Bone, a Holy Instrument of receiving and giving and keeping nothing. Then the words Supreme Being and Human Being made sense to me, and I could also then see that when Einstein ShapeShifted and became a Beam of Light, he was then of Total Service for the Greater Glory of God, and this kind of ShapeShifting is another one of the Eight Natural Indigenous Concepts that we need to activate in order for us to slipslide back into our Natural Flow of Godelution."

Three hands shot up.

"Yes?" I said.

"Isn't ShapeShifting a term used by Native Americans?"

"Yes, and it can also be called SongShifting. You see, when God created the Universe, He/She created One Song, One United Verse, and so it is really all about Energy Frequencies, meaning that each of us comes to Mother Earth with our very own Song, our own unique Vibrational Frequency. Okay, no more, please. I need a little break, "I said, "and then when we come back we can . . . well, understand why it is time in our Godelution for all of us to stop worshipping Jesus and start doing Jesus, because remember Jesus told us that what He did, we would do more?"

"JUST WAIT!" shouted a tall thin priest who was in the back row. "Are you now insinuating you've walked on water?"

"What? Why do you ask this?" I said. I had no idea where he was coming from.

"You just said 'do' Jesus, and Jesus walked on water, and so for us to do Jesus, then we, too, would need to walk on water."

I gripped my forehead. I could feel his frustration from clear across the room and I almost said, "What are you so afraid of?" But I didn't and I closed my eyes, asked for guidance, and I immediately knew deep within me that this guy had been a very abusive priest, and only now, that he was old and fearing death, was he beginning to be haunted by what he'd done

I opened my eyes and said, "Father, it's not too late for you to ask God for forgiveness."

Rage exploded across his face. "How dare you speak to me like this!"

I re-closed my eyes. "Please, Father, understand that it's going to be okay. Truly, God is all about Love and nothing but Love*Amor*. It's our own fears that caused us to come up with all this business of an angry God who's full of wrath, and . . . and we'll get into all this after our little break. Okay, take ten," I said, and quickly walked out of the room. I needed to get to my room as quickly as I could.

# Four

Taking two and three stairs at a time, I ran up to the second story and rushed down the hallway to my room. Going inside and closing the door, I rushed into the bathroom, closed that door, and I took the biggest dump I'd ever taken in my life, and it smelled awful! I had to open the window. My God, what was it that was coming out of me? I guess all these years of holding resentment and anger had fermented into a terrible shit inside of me. I went to the sink and washed my hands and my face with cold water. I guess my mother had been right. It really was affecting me deep inside to have come to see these old nuns and priests. I turned off the water and turned to get a towel and this is when I saw that my dad was standing behind me.

"Hello," I said, reaching around him for a towel.

"*Buenos dias,*" he said with a big smile.

"*Papa,*" I said, drying my hands and face, "I need help. I can't do this alone."

"You're not alone," said another voice,.

I lowered the towel from my face and I saw that my brother Joseph was standing alongside our dad.

"Joseph?" I said. "Oh, wow!"

I hadn't seen my brother in full form since I'd been eight years old and he'd come walking across the water just beyond the breakers with Jesus at his side a few days after he'd passed over.

"We're all here with you," he said. "You have nothing to worry about."

"Really?" I said.

"Yes, just lie down for a few minutes so we can transmit to you," added my brother.

"Transmit? You mean like a radio receives transmissions from their different stations?"

"Yes, through Our Lord we will feed you Heart to Heart and Soul to Soul."

I did as told. I went out of the bathroom, into the bedroom, and fell across my bed and instantly I was out like a light. And when I awoke I felt totally refreshed and ready to go, and looking at the clock by the bed, I could see that I'd only lain down for about eight minutes. It was totally amazing. In just eight minutes it felt as if I'd gained as much rest as a whole night's sleep. But then I remembered that our 8th Sense was Music and Music activated our Soul Computer, and once we moved into this computer, then our 9th Sense, Time, and our 10th Sense, Space, were both relative, and/or disappeared.

I got up. My dad and brother Joseph were both gone, but I knew that they hadn't left me. No, I could still feel them totally here with me. Oh, I was now ready! No more doubt! No more confusion! Now all was smooth sailing inside of me once again. I went whistling down the hallway stairs and I now realized that as a Hollow Bone, a Buffalo Bone, I was being sent Infinite amounts of Love*Amor*, and so of course, I was then supposed to send Infinite Love*Amor* to this priest who'd spoken up.

I went dancing down the hall. My God, I'd never felt better in all my life. Seeing me come into the room, they quickly began taking their seats.

"Good," I said, "I can see that you all came back. Thank you very much. And I want to apologize for my behavior. I had no right to suggest that one of you needed to ask for forgiveness. What I should have done was addressed the question that I'd been asked and that was . . . was I insinuating that I've walked on water. And, well, now the truth is that I didn't know how to answer the question, because—" I blushed. "I had to take a dump, and as it was, I barely made it to my room in time."

People laughed.

"And I'll tell you," I continued, "it turned out being one of the biggest and most awful smelling dumps I've ever taken, and I think it had a lot to do with the fact that I've been holding on to so much crap inside of me for all these years that it had fermented," I added, laughing. "Did anyone else ever have a similar experience?"

Two nuns burst out laughing and nodded their heads, and then the tall, thin priest who'd spoken up, laughed, too.

"I had a big one, too," he said, "and I'm sure that if I hadn't had a big one, I wouldn't have returned."

"Well, I'm very glad that you did," I said, "so we can now address that question of yours. You see, after my dump, my dad and my brother Joseph came to me."

"In spirit?" asked the priest.

"No, yes, I mean, yes, in Spirit, because they've both passed over but they also came to me in full three-dimensional form, and they told me to address your question with a specific question." I breathed. "Tell me, where would we be today if . . . if Peter had not looked down and he had walked side by side with Jesus on water? Eh, where would we all be today?"

I glanced around. My God, the question had really worked. You could hear a pin drop.

"Well, one thing would be for sure," said a nun in the back row who had not spoken, "if Peter hadn't looked down and he'd walked on water alongside Our Lord Jesus, then we wouldn't be as fearful today, because we'd know that if Peter could do this, then maybe we can do it, too."

"We'd all feel closer to Our Lord Jesus," another nun said with tears of joy streaming down her face.

"Everything would be different for us, because we would have been raised to think that walking on water and other such miracles were a normal part of life," said Margaret, the tall, elegant nun.

I smiled and they continued and I could now see why I'd been told to address this question with this specific question. A Miracle was taking place before my very eyes. These nuns were now stepping forward and taking the lead.

"My parents would have felt safe to just love me, and not be so critical," said another nun.

So I continued listening and it was beautiful, then I finally said, "Amen! And I now would like you to know that this was how I was raised by my Yaqui Indian *mamagrande*, and so yes, straight out, I can now tell you that no, I haven't walked on water, but I've done much more. You see, back at one time when we were All, All, All Indigenous People the world over, we knew that ordinary people walked on water when they reached our most perfect human age of 78, so water walking wasn't that big a deal between 78 and 104, which is our normal age for passing."

"What in the world are you now talking about?" asked another priest. "I was just beginning to follow you, and now you throw a whole new wrench into this mess!"

"Here, let me explain," I said, "you see within the Multi-Sensory World of 13 Senses our natural aging process also happens in stages of 13 years. And our first 13 is, of course, puberty, give or take a couple of years. Our second is 26 which is our full male and/or female powers. Our next is at 39, and this is when women stop caring what men think or do and they start coming into their own male powers, and in our society at 39 men start looking at young girls because they start feeling the lessening of their male powers and so they feel the need to prove themselves.

"And then 52 is the big one for both sexes because women stop their periods, give or take two years, and they go through men-o-pause, meaning that they pause before they come into their full male powers. Women actually get a little hair on their upper lip and a few around their nipples, and they become Women of Substance. And at this age you met my two grandmothers and you witnessed them being tough and strong. And men at this point, go through women-o-pause and get unsure and kinder and/or mean. Then at 65, both women and men start to balance out their male and female powers, and then at 78 BINGO! People start living with one foot in This World and the other foot in the Other World, and like I earlier said, to the degree that they accept their Spirituality, to that degree there is no aging between 78 to 104."

"How do you know all this?" asked a priest.

I looked at him and I could see that his question was sincere. "Because," I said to him, "I was educated in our Original Instructions by my Yaqui Indian *mamagrande* before I started school and my parents followed up that education, because they, too, had been home educated by their mothers and grandmothers, and then on the night my dad passed, he told me that he'd be coming back to educate from the University of the Divine once he checked in with his mother, the rest of our *Familia*, and the Grand Masters."

"And we, too, can receive this Divine Education?" asked the same priest.

"Absolutely," I said. "Look about three years back, I was the keynote speaker up in Seattle, and after I'd spoken I went to one of the workshops and this big burly guy with a huge grey beard sprinkled with a lot of red was leading the workshop. His audience was mostly teachers and administrators, and he asked them if they'd ever had the experience of driving in a mall parking lot and had a group of young teenage boys about 14 and 15 walking real slow in front of them. Most of the people raised their hands.

"He laughed and gave a slow strutting gait to demonstrate his point, then said, 'And if you're dumb enough to honk at them, what do they do? They don't get out of your way. Oh, no, they turn and look at you as if you're the one with a problem, and now they walk even slower. So who's had this experience?' With laughter, almost everyone raised their hands. 'And now I want you to know that those boys were doing exactly what they are supposed to be doing,' he said, 'because Socialization is 100s of 1000s of years old, if not millions of years, and Civilization is only 20 to 40,000 years old at best, and we are trying to get boys to conform to Civilization instead of Socialization.'

"Then he explained to us that when young male bear cubs reach this age of about 200 pounds and they start behaving this way, their mothers take them to a spot where they know the bear cub can make it on his own and they leave them and never return. 'At first the male cub gets angry,' he said to us, 'but then as night falls he gets scared, and by daybreak he's so hungry that he starts to fend for himself. And it used to be that when boys got to be 14 and 15 year old, we'd push them out of the nest like the Falcons do, but now in modern times we can't just throw them out of our homes, because we educate our kids for school and college, and not for life, and so they're tough where they should be kind, and wild when they should be cautious. And we parents do this because we have lost our Original Instructions, and don't have a clue how to live a sustainable life or how to pass on information to our children.'

"This was the first time I'd ever heard the term Original Instructions and that there used to be a way to live in harmony with nature instead of conquering the wild and raping our planet. And then he told us that little female bears were kept for about a year longer, so the mother could give her the advanced knowledge of how to be a mother bear, and he told us that he'd learned all this from the Native Americans of the Northwestern United States. I could have listened to that big burly guy all day long. He was wonderful! And he was validating how I'd been raised, telling us things just like my *mamagrande* used to tell me, and he said to us that the ducks and geese knew when to migrate, and salmon knew when to go down river and out to sea and then with their last dying breath they knew how to fight back upstream and spawn.

"And so now after sharing all this background, I can answer your question of how come I know all this. Simply, I came to know all of this because I was raised with the understanding that every day is *otro milagro de Dios*, and so of course, Peter could have walked on water, because when people reached this most perfect age of 78, with one foot on This Side of Living and another on the Other Side of Living, it was then normal to walk on water and perform Daily Miracles.

"And all of you here in this room are at this age and/or approaching this perfect age of 78, and so it's now time for all of you to go for it! And not into retirement, but to go into Inspirement! Because . . . because you are OUR SACRED ELDERS! Look, Miracles are our norm! My whole family and I have done more than just walk on water! We have walked on fire that was measured at 1,200 Fahrenheit, and we've had L.A. rush hour traffic part for us like the Red Sea so we could travel at 60, 70, 90 miles an hour while all the rest of the traffic crept along at 5 and 10 miles an hour, and personally I've walked off a 30 foot rock cliff into thin air, and . . . and God assisted my every step by providing a rock staircase that allowed me to get down from the cliff.

"Remember in *Rain* when my mother Lupe turned into a fern so those renegade soldiers wouldn't rape her and kill her? And do you remember when my dad turned into stone along with the two Yaqui Indians so the prison guards and their pack of dogs didn't tear them to pieces. And both of these Miracles are forms of ShapeShifting, SongShifting, and/or Ghosting, and my parents were able to do them, because my parents had been taught in the old Indian Way how to Breathe in God with their every Breath, and then with the Sacred Holy Breath of God you can do—"

"JUST WAIT!" shouted a priest. "Are you then saying that you didn't write all of these things as metaphors? And your mother Lupe actually turned into a fern?"

"Yes," I said, taking in a deep breath. "This is exactly what I'm saying, and why I got 265 rejections before I got published and . . . and why my New York publisher wanted to bring out *Rain* as fiction, and why my mother—God bless her soul—was willing to mortgage her home, her last possession in the world, so we could buy the rights back from Putnam." Tears came to my eyes. "My mom was in her 80s!" I yelled. "My dad had passed! And still she had the guts, the ovaries, to mortgage her home and . . . and . . . oh, my God!" I said, "Can't you see it? All of Life, *la Vida,* is an ONGOING MIRACLE ONCE WE OPEN UP OUR HEART AND SOUL EYES, and begin to see that we live within Seven Dimensions here in our Sacred Holy Mother Earth!"

I stopped, wiping the tears out of my eye. "And you guys just glimpsed that," I added, "when you saw how different our world would be if Peter had walked on water. So let's not lose that vision that we all just had together, because . . . because what I'm saying is that we all need to get beyond Peter and take Jesus off all the crosses in the world and stop worshipping Him and start being like Him. This was His message. Not that negative story of Him needing to save us from our sins, but instead a positive story of Him coming to Mother Earth to INSPIRE US TO GREATNESS!

"Just imagine what a world we would have if all Christians were into forgiveness, as Our Lord Jesus did on the cross, instead of being so judgmental and into finger pointing, and thinking that their way was the only way. And this is exactly why He came to me when I was eight, so I could learn that when one of our loves passes over, we don't lose them," I said with more tears coming to my eyes, "but instead we gain an even closer relationship with Jesus, and this is also why He came to me in Spain and why He even came to me last night, here at your place, because Jesus has ALWAYS BEEN ALL ABOUT POSITIVE LOVING *amor* AND INCLUSIVE ENERGY!

"You see, it's simply out of date for us to be living in fear of God, and it's out of date to—here, let me tell you a story that will show you that people have really, really, really been walking on water all over the world for eons of timeless time. Okay, ready?" I said, walking away from the podium and getting an empty chair out of the front row and turning it around so I could face them.

"Oh, yeah, this feels so much closer and so much more better," I said, laughing, then I closed my eyes. "In the hallway to my writing room, I have an old black and white picture of Einstein riding a bicycle. He's my hero, because he's happy. Big Big Happy! And this is where we are all now going! Ready? Good. Good. And now just close your eyes, so you don't get distracted and you can slipslide into our Collective Happy Consciousness of the Kingdom of God."

People closed their eyes and I could feel a hush come over the room. And I could also feel that all of the nuns were with me, but the priests, for the most part, were either ready to bolt and/or were shitting square bricks. And sure I understood that I'd take them out of their comfort zone, but I wasn't going to slow down. No, I had to keep going if we were ever going to get anywhere.

"All right," I now said, opening my eyes and looking at the tall, old priest, "and to now address your question about walking on water, or parting the Red Sea, or any of those other old Miracles of the Bible, let me share with you this story about my Great Great Great Great Great Aunt, Mother Of No Specific Child, who, like so many of our Sacred Elders, became a Miracle Maker and a Water Walker at the Blessed Age of 78.

"And so my dad told me that one afternoon our aunt was walking on water from peninsula to peninsula doing her Sacred Holy Healing Work down in the lower part of Mexico when some young Spanish soldiers saw her walking across the water. Instantly they dropped to their knees and started praying, thinking she was of Jesus Christ, but when the old priest found out about this, he screamed blasphemy, and he had her arrested and raped and burned at the stake, so he could prove to these young soldiers that she was of the devil and not of Jesus Christ.

"But it backfired on the old priest." I said, getting out of my chair, "for a young priest named Jose-Maria saw her dignity and purity of love even as she burned, and so he knew that she was, indeed, of Our Lord Jesus Christ. Jose-Maria ripped off his collar and a bunch of the young soldiers joined him and together they united with the local Indians and they revolted against the Church and Spain with SUCH CONVICTION that they almost turned the tide of the European invasion!

"And this, all this, you will, of course, never find in any history book, but this is what my dad told me that his mother *Doña Margarita* told him, and her father *Don Pio* told her, and *Don Pio's* mother told him, and now the big one is that I'd like all of you to know, that from the Other Side, my dad also told me that our Great Great Great Great Great Aunt, Mother Of No Specific Child, was 165 years old when she was arrested, tortured, and then burned at the stake, and so she was totally of Jesus!" I added, with tears streaming down my face.

"And you say your dad told you all of this from the Other Side?" asked a nun.

I nodded. "Yes, he never mentioned her when he was on This Side of Living," I said.

"Why do you think he never did?" asked the same nun.

I laughed. "Look, I had enough trouble believing in the big snake my dad told me about and the dancing clouds of butterflies that my mother spoke to me about, so I'm sure my dad knew that only after he passed over and came to me in my sleep, educating me from the University of the Divine, would I be able to hear him and accept what he told me. And this is what we'll do today after dinner. I'll give you the Tools of Genius that my dad gave me on the night he passed in order for you to receive in your sleep as I've been receiving ever since my dad passed. And all this is being written about in a book called *Beyond Rain of Gold*, but this book will not come out until after *Burro Genius* and *CrazyLoco Love* come out," I added.

"Then you truly believe that your father comes to you in your sleep and it's not just wishful thinking?" asked a priest, with that well practiced little smile of superiority.

And seeing this smile, all the abuses of my childhood came exploding up inside of me and I almost rushed across the room to grab this arrogant old priest by the throat and yank him out of his chair, but I didn't. No, instead I breathed deeply and I closed my eyes, asked for help, and I was immediately told very clear to address his question with a specific question. I opened my eyes.

"Tell me," I said, "do you believe in the Bible?"

"Well, yes, of course, but the Bible is the word of God," he added.

"Okay, I understand that that's what you've been taught to believe, and . . . and particularly because of the word 'the' which is only European based, but we'll get into that later. And right now," I said, "what I'd like to know is did you read *Rain of Gold*?"

His face caved in. Oh, yes, I'd been given the right question.

"Well, not all of it," he said.

"How much is not all of it?" I asked.

"I read the first part of it, and glanced through the rest," he said.

I closed my eyes. "Look," I said, "I didn't become a writer because I wanted to get rich or famous. Hell, I didn't even like books. I became a writer because I made a deal with God." I opened my eyes. "I was 19 years old and I'd just gotten back from Mexico a few days before, and I'd been happy in Mexico. My stomach didn't hurt. But my dad had explained to me that the United States was now our home, that my older uncles and cousins had paid in blood for this country in World War II and Korea and that my two grandmothers were buried here.

"So I returned to the U.S. with my dad and I'd only been here a few days and my stomach was hurting once again with all the racism I saw against Mexicans and Blacks. A hate and rage came exploding up inside of me, especially now that I was no longer ashamed of being Mexican, but actually proud of my Indigenous Ancestry!" I took in a deep breath and blew out fast. "Oh, I was so full of rage that I wanted to kill all of the abusive teachers I've had in public school and also in Catholic school, but then it came to me to pack my rifle and handguns and a few thousand rounds of ammo and get out of town. I got our old ranch truck and took off. I drove east to the rising Father Sun through the back country of Southern California, and then through Las Vegas, Nevada, and St. George, Utah, then north to the southern tip of Idaho, and here I turned east and was going across Wyoming when a herd of antelope ran across the road in front of me. I slammed on my brake, got my Winchester .06 model 70, my .357 Smith and Wesson revolver, and my always-with-me backpack, and took off after the antelope to kill them.

"But then I saw they had yearlings and these little ones looked so innocent. They weren't even afraid of me. In fact, two of them came towards me to see what I was. I guess they'd never seen a human before. And this was when I saw the beautiful snow capped Teton Mountains and I remembered that my *mamagrande* had always told me that it was our job to help *Papito Dios* plant His/Her ongoing Garden of Heaven on Mother Earth. I began to cry, and then screamed, demanding God to tell me how I could plant any Stardust Seeds with all this rage and hate I had inside of me!

"All this I've written in a book called *CrazyLoco Love* which is the second book of the *Burro Genius* trilogy and this is when God spoke to me, not in words, but in flashes of understanding and I learned that God never chose the Jews. No, it was the Jews who chose God when they took their oral story and put it into written form.

"And in that moment of utter clarity, I understood that there were 1000s and 1000s of Bibles that needed to be written from all over Africa, Asia, and the Americas before we could have peace on earth, and that I, myself, had to write my own people's Holy Book, so we, too, could then become the Chosen People of God like the Jews.

"So, please," I now said to this priest, "no more questions, and especially not from you guys who . . . who haven't even read *Rain of Gold* in its entirety, because . . . BECAUSE I DIDN'T WRITE IT!" I screamed. "It came through me just as Einstein's theory came through him and Edison's stuff all came through him and . . . and . . . also understand that I'm not accusing you of being a bad person or anything like that. Hell, I mean, Heaven, I, too, was a Doubting Thomas until my dad passed over in March of 1988, and then he came to me a few months later in New York City in my hotel room, and ever since, he's the one who's been giving me an education straight from Heaven."

I stopped.

I had to sit down. I was shaking, I was so upset. That old priest had no idea how close I'd came to rushing across the room and slapping that little grin off his face.

"And he's right," said Sister Mary. "You wouldn't even be asking these questions if you'd read the book as we asked you to!!" She was pissed!

"I suggest that we listen to Victor. May I call you Victor?" asked Margaret.

"Of course," I said.

"I suggest that we listen to him as if he's teaching us how to fly a plane," she said, "or as if he's guiding us through this new world of computers."

"Thank you," I said, calming down and wiping the tears out of my eyes. "Thank you very much, and to learn how to fly and/or use a computer there is an entire new language of concepts that we need to learn. Thank you, sister. Your suggestion will be a big help."

"Call me *Margarita*, if you don't mind. *Margarita* like your grandmother."

I smiled. "Of course, *Margarita*," I said to her.

Six hands shot up.

"No, please, no more questions," I said, laughing. "In fact, no more words, no more talking. Let's all just take a little break, so we can digest all this within our own Kingdom of God, then BOOM! We'll come back and go for it ALL THE WAY BACK TO THE FUTURE!"

"It's almost lunch time," announced Father James, standing up, "so why don't we just call it quits for this morning's session."

And as I went out of the room, out of the corner of my eye, I saw that Father James was aglow with a bright and yet soft golden light. Oh, my God, this priest was an Archangel!

# Five

---

This time I did not go to my room. I went out the door towards the lake, and the honkers immediately greeted me with their honking. I laughed and said, "hello" to them and continued down the grassy knoll to the lake. Oh, the air smelled so crisp and fresh, and I needed to get away from everyone. I'd never expected this whole thing to go as it had gone. Wow! I'd never thought I'd get into all this heavy stuff, especially not right away. I thought that I'd first start out by telling these old nuns and priests why it was that I'd first fallen in love with the Holy Roman Catholic Church at St. Patrick's in Carlsbad, with the smells and happy sounds of the altar boys pretending to sing back to the old half deaf priest in Latin, but they were actually singing back in Spanish about the best way to cook wild turkey and Mexican green sauce.

And then I figured that after saying this to the old nun and priests and getting them laughing, I'd tell them why I'd quit being a Catholic with a capital 'C' and I was now a catholic with a small 'c', and how I felt so much closer to God by having done this. And so I was walking along thinking all this and feeling happy and enjoying the sight of all the honkers and deer and the beautiful clear blue water, when that youngish priest came running up to me. He was all out of breath.

"Oh, I'm so glad to catch you alone," he said. "I'm Mark," he added.

"You're a priest, aren't you?" I said, because priests normally didn't give you their first name when they introduced themselves.

"Well, yes, but not for much longer," he said. "You see, I'm leaving the priesthood and getting married."

"Married?" I said.

"Yes, I, too, proposed to a nun," he said.

"Oh," I said, laughing, "then this explains why I've seen you smiling so much. You're in love."

"Yes, I'm definitely in love," he said. "And I've never been in love like this before."

"And it feels wonderful, eh?"

"Oh, yes, of course, and best of all, I don't feel guilty about being in love and she doesn't either. But, well, it was really very difficult for both of us at first, because of all the pressure that was put on us."

"I can only imagine," I said, putting my hand on his shoulder, "that took a lot of guts. Why do you think they call it 'falling in love', eh? It's scary."

He laughed. "You're right. It has been the scariest thing I've ever done in my life," he said. "The feelings I was feeling were so powerful and confusing and real!"

"Exactly, because for a person to truly allow himself to fall in love, not only takes a leap of faith as much as walking on water, but then to walk down the aisle to join hands in marriage is a commitment that takes guts way beyond all reasonable comprehension."

"Well, talking about guts," he said, "we read in *People Magazine* about you buying the rights back to *Rain of Gold* from your publisher."

"Yes," I said, "and it all got started with an article in *Publisher's Weekly* where Joe Baro – something wrote about my old mother mortgaging her home so we could buy the rights of *Rain of Gold* back from Putnam, my New York publisher, for $75,000, and how I then got blackballed all over New York."

"And you ended up going with a small press at the University of Houston," he said.

"Exactly," I said, "for 1,500 dollars, and this is when I become a Born Again Texan and reporters came at me from across the country. Everyone was astonished. But my *familia* and I weren't. My parents' story wasn't fiction," I added. "But now, please, no more about that. Tell me about you and this nun. What's her name?"

"*Josefina*," he said, pronouncing her name with a beautiful *Latino* song-like softness.

"*Josefina*," I repeated, but I couldn't quite say it as romantically.

We continued walking on the grass along the edge of the lake and he told me how Sister Josefina and he had met while working together in Ecuador, and they'd been very good friends for nearly a year, but then at an All Saints Day celebration, which were always such large events throughout Latin America, they'd been so happy and excited together that it had frightened them.

"I'll never forget," he said, "it was a full moon and there were fireworks and kids running all around us and something happened to us, and we just looked at each other in a way that we'd never looked at each other before. So for the next few days we both avoided each other, but then I began to dream of *Josefina* in a way that I'd never dreamed of her previously. And a few years before, I would have gone to confession and asked for forgiveness for the kind of dreams I was having, but not now. Now I knew deep in my heart and soul that these dreams weren't a sin, but instead wonderful and a whole new way of viewing love and life itself, and . . . . and I then realized I could no longer be a priest. And strangely enough, this was also when I began to understand that Jesus, as a man, must've loved Mary Magdalene. How could He have not? Because my love for *Josefina* felt so natural and good."

He stopped talking and I saw he had tears running down his face, so I took him by his shoulders and turned him around and hugged him. He was trembling and having trouble breathing. My God, these dreams that he'd had for *Josefina* must've frightened him to no end. He hugged me back, squeezing me with all his might.

"Good," I said, "good. We all need to hug."

"Yes, I can see that now," he said, releasing me, "but I couldn't at first. Oh, all year I'd seen *Josefina* be the kindest, most loving human I'd ever met, just as you spoke about your own little nun. And so finally I, too, got up the nerve to go to her and tell her of my love for her and that I was leaving the priesthood, because I would never again feel ashamed of the feelings that I had for her. She began to cry, saying that she felt the same way about me, and that she, too, would not allow anyone to make her feel ashamed of her feelings, and this was when we took each other in our arms in a whole new way and . . . and then we announced our intent of leaving and getting married and we were, well, imme- diately separated and I was sent here and . . . and she was sent to a convent."

"What? You mean you've lost her?" I asked.

"Oh, no," he said. "We were told that we'd have to be six months apart, so we could pray and ask for guidance before we can legally leave the Church and marry. And it's now been 5 months, 16 days, and 12 hours, and 36 minutes," he said, glancing at his wristwatch with the biggest smile I'd ever seen on a human being.

"Congratulations!" I said. "Good for you!"

"By the way," he said, "it's important that you know that Father James is the only one who knows why I'm here. All the rest think I had a nervous breakdown, instead of a LOVE BURST!" he shouted with joy.

We hugged again, holding each other a long time, then we continued walking along the lake together.

"Do you know where *Josefina* is?" I asked.

"I think so."

"Then you haven't been in contact with her?"

"Oh, no, like I said that's part of our deal, that we won't make contact with each other for six months."

I stopped walking and turned to face him. "Okay, all that sounds good and, well, reasonable," I said. "And yet, I hate to say this, but you can't trust these decision-makers of the Church, especially the higher and higher they get up in the politics of the Church." I took in a deep breath. "Has *Josefina* read *Rain of Gold?*" I asked.

He shook his head. "No, we'd never heard of you or any of your books. I only found out about you when I arrived here and I heard all these nuns talking so excited, about *Rain of Gold.*"

"Well, I really do suggest that you get a copy of *Rain* sent to her immediately. You see, I always tell young women that when they finally find a guy that they're really interested in to have him read *Rain of Gold,* and if he doesn't love the book to dump him, because *Rain* is all about strong women, and shows men and the whole world what it means to be a strong woman of substance through war, through peace, through all the twist and turns of life."

"And you think it will help *Josefina* not to lose faith."

"Exactly," I said, "because they did everything they could to break the little nun that I'd proposed to, and I'm sure that they are now trying to do that to *Josefina*. My God, in just a few weeks Sister Theresa had aged years and lost so much weight it was frightening. I strongly recommend that you find out where *Josefina* is and send her a copy of *Rain of Gold*. But, "I added, "do not go through normal channels. Did she have any close nun friends?"

"Oh, yes, she was extremely loved."

"Well, then contact them. No, wait. Don't contact her best friend *Sophia*, I do believe. Contact her other best friend *Maria*."

"How do you know their names?" he asked.

"Look," I said, laughing, "once we get out of the prison of our limiting 5 sensory perception and we access our Kingdom of God with our Multi-Sensory Perception of our Full Natural 13 Senses, all of us then Know Everything! Truly, Jesus Knew what He was talking about when He said that we each have the Kingdom of God within us. Just think about it. Within the Kingdom of God is Everything, Past, Present, Future, and so then—"

"We Know Everything," he said, grinning.

"Exactly, but with 5 senses we don't have the tools with which to access all we Know deep inside of ourselves, and with our Full Natural 13 Senses, we do."

"Then this is how you Know what Einstein said about not riding on a beam of light, but that he became a Beam of Light?"

"Exactly," I said. "Albert is one of the Grand Masters that I'm now in contact with ever since my dad passed over. You see, when one of our loved ones passes over, we don't lose them. What actually happens is that we gain a stronger access to the Other Side of Living, and the Church used to acknowledge this until the 4th Century when they then decided to do away with reincarnation and all of our other Natural Knowledge that comes to us with our Multi-Sensory Perception."

"Then are you saying that you believe in reincarnation?"

"No, belief is a weak word, so I don't believe in anything anymore."

"I don't understand."

"Look, you don't believe that tomatoes taste good. You Know that tomatoes taste good. You don't believe in taking a crap. You Know you need to crap."

"Well, yes, but a tomato is something we can see and feel, and needing to crap is a function that our body tells us."

"Exactly," I said, "and once we move out of our prison of our limiting 5 senses, and into our Natural Multi-Sensory Perception of 13 Senses, then we stop believing and start Knowing with a capital K."

"Even God?"

"Most especially God," I said. "My two grandmothers didn't believe in God. They Knew God and they lived with the Almighty with their every Breath. But I also didn't fully understand this until I met two Native American educators in Nashville, Tennessee back in 1992 at the National

Library Convention. And this is when I stopped believing and began to either Know something or not Know. Like I don't believe in God anymore, I Know God, and so just like my *mamagrandes* I, too, now live with the Almighty with my every Breath. And about reincarnation; no, I no longer believe in reincarnation. I Know reincarnation, here, deep inside of me."

"You know reincarnation?"

"Yes, I Know . . . that I've had 15 lifetimes on this planet and that this is only my second time as a male, and I also Know that I've had 1000s and 1000s of past lives on our other Six Sister Planets."

"Really? You Know this?"

"Yes, I absolutely Know this!"

"And you think, I mean, you Know that all of us can reach this Level of Knowingness?"

"Of course, we all have the Kingdom of God within us," I said.

He nodded and nodded again and said nothing more as we continued walking alongside the lake, listening to the little waves slapping up against the shoreline.

"You know," he said after a while, "these things you've been telling us are beginning to make sense, and I can now see they were in *Rain of Gold* between the lines, but I, well, hadn't been able to see them." He stopped, turned to me, and asked, "Did you do this deliberately."

"Oh, yes," I said, laughing. "After 265 rejections I Knew that I had to do what old Hemingway suggested and keep 7/8 of what I was saying under water or I'd never get published."

"I see, I see," he said. "You know what really resonated within me was when you said that our planet is a very emotional and sexual driven planet. I mean, ever since I admitted to myself that . . . that I was also physically in love with *Josefina* and not just spiritually, it's been so complete feeling within me that, well, I now see everything differently."

"Go on," I said.

"Well, it's like I now see everything alive and full of joy," he said, laughing. "I swear that when I first arrived here, the geese came rushing up to me and they congratulated me on being in love. I Know this sounds crazy, but it's true! That's what it felt like, and then the trees and the grass were all happy to see me, too!" He spun around, shouting with joy. "IT'S LIKE THE WHOLE WORLD KNOWS I'M IN LOVE AND IS SO BEAUTIFUL AND HAPPY FOR ME! And this is when I just KNEW that Jesus had been in love with Magdalene, and so, of course, they'd made love and had children! How could they not have, eh?"

I was laughing and laughing. "You're absolutely right, and they did have kids, and we'll get into all of that too, because this is, indeed, the most emotional and sensually driven planet and of our Six Sister Planets, and so it is our duty to live with all our Heart and Soul and Body and Mind, and this is how we finally have no Illusions of Separation and/or Mortality, and start Living on the Active Side of Eternity!"

"Then you believe–I mean, Know that believing is, well, in fact, misleading?"

"You tell me," I said. "You have your own Kingdom of God within you, and you're the one who's now in love, and with Love*Amor*, you are Totally Connected. You see, believing insinuates not Knowing, and as soon as you get people to not trust their Inner All-Knowingness, then this is when we become easy targets for manipulation by man-made institutions, because we've lost our Natural Direct Connection to God."

"I see," he said, nodding, "I see."

And once again he said nothing more and we continued walking and could see it in his eyes, he was letting all this soak in. This was a big one. To move from believing to Knowing had taken me years.

"Will you be talking to us about this?" he asked.

"About Knowing?"

He nodded.

"You tell me," I said.

He laughed. "I think you should. NO, I KNOW YOU SHOULD! I'm sure a lot of us are tired of all the manipulation that was done to us!"

I burst out laughing with *carcajadas*. I liked this guy. I really did. I was so happy that he'd chased me down.

"Okay," I said. "I'll go for it!"

And it was now time for us to head back, so we could eat lunch.

"So tell me," I said, "what is your relationship with Father James?"

"What do you mean by that?"

"Well, you two seem very close, so I was wondering if—"

"If we're gay? Yes, a lot of the others think that, but we're not," he said.

"Well, that wasn't what I was referring to," I said. "I was wondering if you Know that he's an Angel, actually a—"

"Oh, yes, I Know that," he said. "Of course, James is an Angel, if it wasn't for him I might have lost faith in my love."

"Then have you seen his glow?" I asked.

"Seen him glow? You mean, glow with Light like an actual Angel?"

"An Archangel," I said.

"Really? You're saying Father James is an Archangel?"

"Yes."

"Well, it doesn't surprise me," he said. "In fact, it actually makes sense. Without his help our good nuns would have never been able to bring you here. The priest, as I assume you've guessed, were not that keen to have you come."

It was my time to nod and nod again. "Oh, I see," I said. "I get it now."

"So how do you know that James is an Archangel? Have you seen others?" he asked.

"Yes, in Chicago I met this chubby *Latino* teacher, who looked a lot like the comic Paul Rodriguez, who was an Archangel."

"Really?"

"Yes."

"And what is the difference between an Angel and an Archangel? They're both God's Messengers of Light, correct?"

"Yes, you are right, and what I've seen," I said, "is that an Archangel's Light is almost as bright as the Golden Light I saw surrounding Jesus when He came to me in Spain."

"Really?"

"Well, maybe not that bright, but still highly illuminating."

"So, then, was your grandmother *Doña Margarita*, an Angel or was she an Archangel?"

I laughed. "Why do you ask that?"

"Well, the relationship that she had with the Virgin Mary, and the way Jesus would come to them in Church, but then she'd tell Jesus to keep still and not interrupt the conversation that she was having with His mother, made me think this."

I laughed again. "No, she wasn't really an Angel or an Archangel. She, like Walt Disney, Emerson, Einstein, Cervantes, and Confucius and Moses, was a Grand Master, and so this allowed her take on leadership, which Angels, and especially Archangels, are not allowed to do."

"Really?"

"Yes, that Archangel in Chicago explained all this to me. He was a high school teacher and I asked him if he was going to become a principal or a school district superintendent and really make a big difference in the Chicago school system, and he said no. That as an Archangel he could only illuminate but not lead and/or interfere, that we, humans, had to come into our own Enlightenment, and this was why Jesus hadn't brought down 10,000 Angels and destroyed the whole Roman Empire, but instead He'd given Illumination."

"I see, I see," said Mark. "And is this what your Great Great Great Great Great Aunt, Mothers Of No Specific Child, was doing when she allowed them to rape her and burned her at the stake?"

"Exactly," I said with tears coming to my eyes, "because she was Totally of Jesus, so she, too, could've brought forth all her Miraculous Healing Powers and the Heavens would've opened up with Legions of Angels but she chose not to do this just as Our Lord Jesus chose not to. And what They both did was Inspire us to Greatness! And Jose-Maria saw this, and so did many of the young soldiers."

"But the old priest couldn't see it," said Mark, "because he saw all the Native Americans as ignorant savages, and, well, I need to admit that I, too, can relate to that. When I first arrived in Ecuador I, too, couldn't see the purity of love for God that the local native people demonstrated so naturally. Then when I did, I began falling in love with *Josefina*. She and her fellow native nuns were just so pure in their love for God. Will you talk to us about this?" he asked.

"You tell me?" I said.

He laughed. "Well, I guess it will depend on our availability."

I laughed. "Exactly," I said. "I never Know what I'm going to do and/or say. My Spiritual Guides guide me moment by moment. And also I don't want those guys in the back to decide to burn me at that stake."

He laughed. "Well, anyway, when you said that this is a very emotional and sexual driven planet, then a lot of the feelings I've been having started to falling in place and – oh, I'm just looking forward to being married so much! I'm 40 years old and I'm a virgin! And I no longer want to be a virgin!"

"How old is *Josefina?*"

"She'll be 33 next week, and oh, boy, are we going to make babies!"

I put my arm around his shoulder. "Good for you! And I'd like you to Know that not just the geese and the trees and all of Creation here on our planet are root-ing for you, but also Our Star Cousins from Our Six Sister Planets are rooting you, too. You see, Our Beloved Mother Earth is the Hawaii of our planets, and all Six Sisters are waiting for us to open up Our HeartEyes and

SoulEyes with Love*Amor,* so that they can then flood us with MIRACULOUS HEALING POWERS!"

"OH, WOW! You're right! I can feel it! Because once I let myself fall totally wildly in love *con mi amor, Josefina,* then it was like the Heavens parted for me and I was so happy! And my Dreams became Adventures of Spirit like I'd been Reconnected Directly to Creation itself!

"Yes! Yes! Yes!" I said. "And it all begins with us allowing ourselves to fall madly unconditionally in Love*Amor*!"

"Yes, I can feel it! And this is exactly why *Josefina* and I will not allow anyone to make us feel ashamed of these wild feelings that we're feeling for each other!"

"Absolutely! Anytime, anywhere, any way two people fall in Love*Amor,* they are doing God's Holy Work on Mother Earth! Because only through Joy and Being Happy! BIG BIG HAPPY do we help the Almighty spread His/Her Love*Amor* throughout the WHOLE ENTIRE UNIVERSE!"

And saying this, I took Father Mark in my arms, and jerked him close, kissing him on one cheek and then on the other, and he didn't resist. In fact, he kissed me back on both cheeks, too. Then arm in arm the two of us continued up the grassy knoll through the honkers and deer and we could see there was a group of nuns and two priests waiting for us at the outside patio of the huge mansion. And they looked very excited to see us coming up the knoll. I guess that they'd been watching Mark and me. Coming into the patio, Sister Mary came rushing at me.

"I want one of those hugs, too!" she yelled, grabbing me in her arms.

And she hugged me with her whole body and then gave me a big long juicy kiss on each cheek.

"Oh, that was fun!" she said. "I haven't kissed like that since I was a teenager! And it felt wonderful back then, too!"

*Margarita* and two other nuns were in line and they, too, hugged me and kissed me, but not quite with the fire that Sister Mary had kissed me.

"How about you guys," I said to the two priests. "Come on, just a hug. We don't need to kiss."

And it surprised me. It was the tall thin priest who came forward.

"I guess, I'll take a hug," he said.

And so we hugged, but he made sure to keep his lower body completely away from me, and then we all went inside to have lunch. And the honkers, they could feel the Love*Amor* that had come to us, and they now came honking up to the patio with great sound and excitement. Mark had been right. The birds, the trees, the grass, the lake, all of Creation could feel the Vibrational Frequency of our Love*Amor!*

# BOOK TWO

# Six

After lunch I went to my room and took a little nap, and then when I awoke I was so happy! BIG BIG HAPPY that I'd listened to my mother and I'd come to see these old nuns and priest. I got up, washed my face, and went dancing down the hallway to the stairs.

"Thank You, God!" I said. "Thank You, Lord God! And thank you, *mama*, and thank you, *papa*, on the Other Side! I'm ready! I'm all ready, so let's just go for it!"

And when I walked into the room where we were having our event, I saw that my dad and my brother Joseph and a whole bunch of other relatives and Grand Masters from the Spirit World were over by the windows facing the lake. I nodded to them and they all nodded back to me, and then Bossy Bill Shakespeare stepped forward.

"Oh, no, Bill," I said to him. "This isn't your show." Then I turned to Cervantes and said, "Please handle Bill for me. I don't want him trying to take over like he does."

"I could save you years of writing, if you'd just trust me," said Bossy Bill.

"Bill!" I said with authority. "We've been through this with you a dozen times! And I'm saying no to you now just like I said no to you 30 years ago in Ocean Beach!"

"Excuse me," I heard someone say behind me, "but who are you talking to?"

I turned and saw that all the nuns and priests were staring at me, except Father James, who was smiling this huge smile full of mischief like saying, "Okay, *amigo*, now how are you going to get out of this one?"

And I knew what he was talking about because I was fairly sure that only he and I could see these individuals from the Other Side of Living.

I took in a deep breath, and decided just to go for it all the way. "I'm talking to Bossy Bill Shakespeare," I said to the nuns and priests. "You see, ever since I took my oath to become a writer as great as Homer and/ or greater, Bossy Bill has been a pain in the ass, coming to me and insisting that he can help me to become a great writer. But I always brush him off, explaining to him that I prefer to get help from Cervantes, Azuela, Dostoyevsky, Tolstoy, and Anne Frank."

"But why would you refuse William Shakespeare's help if he is, in fact, coming to you and making himself available to you?" asked a priest.

I took in a deep breath and closed my eyes. "Because," I said, "when Bossy Bill wrote, 'To be or not to be' and he said that this was the question, he was barking up the right tree, but he'd missed the whole point, because to be or not to be is the answer. Not the question." And besides I find him to be arrogant and too much in his intellectual head and so I prefer Anne Frank who's centered in her heart."

I stopped. I could see that half of the nuns and priests were staring at me as if I'd just gone off the deep end. But then Father James saved the day. He started clapping vigorously!

"Wonderful!" he said. "Wonderful! And so should we put out more chairs? How many of these guests from Heaven are here with us?" he asked.

I had to smile. He really Knew his stuff. "Right now we have about a dozen," I said, "but I can see that others are coming."

"Well, we'll just put out two dozen more chairs," said Father James. "Tell me, are we going to be able to see them, too, I hope."

"Yes, I'm sure you will," I said, smiling, "especially after you sleep tonight, and tomorrow awake with the understanding that *mañana es,* indeed, *otro milagro de Dios,* that tomorrow is, indeed, another miracle from God."

Quickly, the priests and nuns brought out the other chairs and set them up, and this was when Father James came up to me and he was glowing.

"You're doing fine," he said to me quietly. "You're doing fine."

"Thanks for the help," I said to him.

"That's what I'm here for," he said.

"Yes, I learned that in Chicago," I said.

"All right, now continue," he said.

And he was in Full Illumination as he turned and went to sit down with the others. And this was when I Knew for sure that Mark and the other priests and nuns couldn't see Father James glow anymore than they could see our guests from the Spirit World. And yet all the nuns and priests were smiling and looking very happy. Yes, they could "feel" the Other Side of Living, but they couldn't "see" it until they'd Activated their Kingdom of God, and then to the degree that they allowed themselves to open up their HeartEyes and SoulEyes to this degree they'd Awaken.

"Okay," I said, "any questions?"

Our Spiritual Guests had taken their chairs along with the nuns and priests. Eight hands shot up.

"Okay, you in the back," I said.

"I thought we had freewill," said this priest, "so then how can the Spirit World dictate to us?"

"You're right, we do have free will," I said, "but it's like choosing up teams to play baseball, and so once I made my deal with God up on that tall *mesa* out in the middle of nowhere in Wyoming, that was it. There is no turning back once you chose your team, because to choose, I'd put my whole Heart and Soul into our Deal, telling God if He didn't chicken-out on me, then I'd never chicken-out on Him."

"Just like Our Beloved Mother Teresa," said Mary with Holy Reverence as she made the sign of the cross over herself.

"Yes, exactly," I said, "and so 265 rejections was no big deal for me. My God, both of my grandmothers had suffered incredible starvation and gave witness to their children being slaughtered, so the deal I made with was FOREVER!" I added.

"And you were 19 years old when you made this deal with the Almighty?"

I wiped the tears out of my eyes. "Yes," I said, "I was 19 when I had that . . . that conversation with God, but then getting back home from Wyoming, it was like I'd lost that Inner Voice I'd heard so well out in the wilds. And this was when it came to me that I had to get away from *mi familia* and friends, who all thought I'd gone off the deep end, because they had absolutely no comprehension of what it meant to me to become a writer in partnership with God.

"Look, I'm also sure that the same thing happened to a lot of you with your friends and family who probably thought you'd lost it when you first informed them that you were going to become nuns and priests."

Many of the nuns and priest nodded.

"So what did you do to re-establish your conversation with God?" asked another priest.

I took in a big deep breath. "I decided to go six months without speaking, but to accomplish this, I also realized that I had to go to a place where no one knew me, and yet I wanted to stay close to the ocean, because *Nuestra Madre Pacifica* had always felt like my connection to God. So I rented a beach shack in Ocean Beach, and I was ready to go the rest of my life without speaking if need be, but then . . . then it was, I guess, somewhere in the middle of the 4th month when I was walking along the seashore late one night and the Heavens were full of Stars, that it came to me that it was, indeed, the darkness of the night that allowed us to see the stars.

"I stopped, I'll never forget, and I looked up at all the Stars, *mi familia*, as my *mamagrande* had taught me, and now, for the first time, I saw that the Darkness was Holy and so Beautiful because it was what gave Life to Stars! Tears came to my eyes, and I went back to my shack that night and I was listening to Sonny Rollins and his long pauses between the notes when it also came to me with such utter clarity that it was the Silence between the notes that gave Life to Music!

"I LEAPED UP SCREAMING! I'll never forget, I screamed and screamed and went running back to the beach, stripped off all my clothes, and went racing into the surf and the waves! For I could now clearly see that God had never stopped speaking to me! That He was, indeed, speaking to all of us through the Darkness of the

Night that allowed us to see the Stars, *nuestra familia*, and He was also speaking to us through the Great Infinite Silence that gave Life to our Music!

"I swam out past the waves and I could now understand that God in His Infinite Wisdom had such Trust in me along with my Guardian Angel that He was Totally, Totally, Totally leaving it up to me to start making my own Holy Notes, my own Holy Music, for God needed us as much as we needed Him/Her so we could help plant His/Her ongoing Holy Sacred Garden here on Mother Earth just like my *mamagrande* HAD ALWAYS TOLD ME!

"And so, of course, it was that day at daybreak on the 16th of September 1960 with the Father Sun, the Right Eye of God, coming up with all His Glory that I started writing, and I've been writing ever since NON-STOP to this day some 40-some years later! And it was Sonny Rollins with his wondrous long pauses of Silence between his Notes that opened up the Heavens for me, and now all of *mi familia* and the Grand Masters began coming to me each morning at about 2 a.m. when I began to write. And everything was going fine and wonderful until . . . until Bossy Bill tried to take over, promising me all these great riches. And I'm sure he was right, but not for me. Still Shakespeare was so insistent, that I finally quit arguing with him and just started putting up signs at the door of my writing room and in the kitchen that simply said, 'Keep Out, Bill!'"

"You really did that?" asked a nun, giggling with laughter.

"Did what?" I asked.

"Put up signs that said, 'Keep Out, Bill!'"

"Oh, yes, sure, I had to. You can't fool around with the Spirit World."

By now a lot of people were laughing.

But then one priest became very serious looking, and said, "Are you insinuating that William Shakespeare is an evil spirit?"

"Oh, no, not at all," I said. "Bill is fine and good, but just not for me. Look, just like you guys read in *Rain of Gold* that my grandmother *Doña Margarita* finally had to tell Jesus to keep still, because she was having a woman-to-woman conversation with His Mother, I had to do the same with Bossy Bill, or he would have taken over."

"Excuse me, but I'd assumed that scene with your grandmother was symbolism," said another priest.

"Oh, no, I don't write symbolism," I said. "I write stark raw reality within the perception of Our Full Natural 13 Senses."

"Will you explain this?"

"Yes, of course," I said, laughing, "but first let me tell you what happened a few years back when I shared this conversation about Bossy Bill with a bunch of university professors. After my talk an older black woman ran to get in the elevator with me and she was all smiles until the doors closed. Then she started screaming and hitting me with this huge book of the collective works of Bossy Bill, calling me all kinds of names. And she was strong and that book must've weighed half a ton, and I kept pushing buttons to try to get out of the elevator before she killed me.

"You see," I said, "English, the English language, has become a religion on its own, and has all but taken over the whole world, and Shakespeare's writing encourages this to such a degree that we now brag about "English

Only" in our country, and this is not just dangerous, but self destructive because . . . because English is the only language that I know of that capitalizes the word 'I'. Spanish doesn't capitalize 'yo' unless you're a California surfer and you drive a Toyota pickup and you block out the first two letters and the last two letters of the word Toyota on the back of your tailgate.

"And then add to this what I've already mentioned that only European based-languages have the word 'the' and you have a very arrogant self-serving language in English. Truly, everywhere I go I tell people that our only hope for this nation is to start learning other languages and not just European based, because now with modern brain scans we are beginning to understand that when you learn a second language you don't just learn more words. No, you actually start accessing other parts of the brain, and a third language causes flexibility of the brain and you then end up having a much better chance of not ending up with Alzheimer's.

"So I told this group of professors that Shakespeare was out-of-date and it was time for us to start learning African Languages, and Asian and Native American languages, and so this woman who was African, I'd thought she'd gotten into the elevator to congratulate me. Not kill me," I said, laughing. "And what I guess really pissed her off was when I'd said Shakespearian plays were also totally out-of-date, and what we needed was for *Roots* by Alex Haley to be made into a musical and/or a Broadway play every 10 or 15 years like they do for all these other American classics. Truly, it's no accident that even that African professor became enraged. Everywhere I now give talks, I find out that high school kids have never even heard of *Roots* and of Kunta Kinte being raised up to the Stars in that fantastic scene that still sends chills up and down my spine, because this was what was done to me by my *mamagrande!* Truly, we need to break loose from the prison of 'English Only'."

"That makes sense to me," said Father Mark. "It wasn't until I'd been down in Ecuador for nearly six months and spoke Spanish pretty well and also a good deal of the local Native language that I could begin to open my eyes and see that there is a whole world out there beyond English."

"Exactly," I said, "and even Bossy Bill is now beginning to acknowledge this, because he has become good friends with Alex Haley. In fact, they're now *compadres.*"

"Oh, godfathers," said Mark.

"Yes," I said. "Look, the most important thing for all of us to remember on This Side and/or on the Other Side of Living is to Trust with a capital 'T', because we can't access the Kingdom of God that we have within us until we have the understanding and the Complete Trust that we live in a wonderful loving Universe. As Henry Miller so well said in his book *Tropic of Capricorn,* 'Once you give up the ghost everything follows with dead certainty, even in the midst of chaos,' then he took off in an Arthur Rimbaud- like journey."

Then one of our Spiritual Guests spoke up, but I didn't quite get what he'd said. And when he spoke again with his heavy Brooklyn accent, I laughed, because I now knew that it was Henry Miller himself, whom I'd once met at his home out at the Pacific Palisades near Malibu in Los Angeles.

"Okay, Mr. Miller," I now said. "I'm listening. Please, go ahead. Yes, of course, I hear you, and I was going to get into all that tomorrow, but not now. All right, all right, *papa*, I hear you, too."

"What's going on?" asked a priest.

"Well, Mr. Miller and my dad and now even Bossy Bill and Azuela are telling me to move you guys into Geniusing right now, and then I can start sharing with you the Eight Indigenous Concepts that will free us from the past, so then we automatically slipslide into World Harmony and Peace and Abundance for All as has already been done on our other Six Sister Planets. And they're also telling me to inform all of you that back at one time our Six Sister Planets were even more lost and violent than us, and so we can do this here on Mother Earth, because, remember, we, Human People, are Hollow Bones, Buffalo Bones, Holy Instruments for helping the Almighty spread His/Her Love *Amor* throughout the Universe!"

I took in a big deep breath. "Okay, fasten your seatbelts, because the first question we need to address before we can climb aboard Our Spaceship and BLAST OFF into Inner Outer Space is . . . is, are you a genius? Then after that the next question is how many of you can imagine, just imagine, the possibility of World Harmony and Peace and Abundance for All for the next 5,000 years, even with all the problems that we have going on. Ready? And if you can see it, if you can imagine it, then please raise up your hand for each of these two questions."

"You're joking, right?" said a priest.

"Oh, no, not at all," I said. "In fact, these two are the normal questions I ask everywhere I go, and I can now see that I shouldn't have let you guys off the hook and asked you these two questions right from the start. You see, when I ask kindergarten kids these questions, they immediately all raise their hands to both of these questions, and one little *vato*-kid in Texas even flipped on the floor and raised up both feet and both hands, and I said to him, 'So you think you're a genius, eh?'

"'Yes,' he said, 'I'm really good!'

"'What makes you think you're so good?' I asked.

"'Look at my finger painting,' he said.

"I walked over and looked, then said, 'That's as good as any Picasso!'

"'Yes,' he said, 'because I'M A GENIUS!'

"'Okay,' I said, 'and since you're a genius, do you as a genius think we can have World Wide Harmony and Peace and Abundance for All for 5,000 years, even with all the *problemas* that we have going on?'

"'Sure,' he quickly said.

"'And why do you think this?'

"'Because it's MORE FUN!' he shouted."

And having shared this little story, I laughed and laughed, figuring that all the nuns and priests would laugh along with me, but they didn't. One priest immediately spoke up full of frustration.

"Yes, but that child had no idea what genius means or any comprehension of what it means to have world peace!" he said.

I closed my eyes. "And you do, eh?" I said. "Tell me, have you ever looked up the word 'genius' in the dictionary?"

"No, I haven't," he said.

I opened my eyes. "Well, then I'll tell you that kid in kinder-garden knew more about genius than you do. For nearly 20 years I've been asking people these two questions and adults are all so quick to say that children don't know what genius means, and yet not once have I found any adult who has looked up the word and remembers what genius means.

"And this is no accident, because by first grade there are less geniuses, by second and third grade less and less, and by fourth grade there are no geniuses left, and then in the seventh grade the girls who get straight 'A's raise their hands and the boys who are bored stiff at school raise their hands sarcastically. You see, our educational system crushes genius and replaces it with kids who have learned how to cram for tests and regurgitate what they've been taught, and that's not genius.

"Okay, no more of this," I said, taking in a deep breath, "now let's just go for it like kinder-garden kids and have fun! BIG BIG FUN! Okay, ready? And so I now ask all of you here, who's a genius? Come on, go for it!"

Two nuns raised their hands.

"Okay, good, not bad," I said. "And I fully realized that all of you were educated to not brag, to not walk down the center of a hallway, but to walk along the edge of the hallway, so people wouldn't think that you are being arrogant, but . . . and this is a big 'but', being a genius, admitting to geniusing, isn't about arrogance. No, it's about Activating the Kingdom of God that Jesus so wisely told us is within each of us. So now come on! Go for it! Are you a genius?"

Still it was only the same two nuns who raised their hands. Henry Miller had been right. This question had certainly taken these old nuns and priests out of their comfort zone.

"COME ON!" I said again. "Once you give up the ghost, then all the illusions, all the fears and expectations and all the negative crap that's been fed to us since birth, dissolves, disappears, and then everything follows with wonderful dead certainty, even in the midst of chaos!"

Still no one else raised their hand.

"Excuse me," said the tall, elegant nun in the front row who'd said she'd been a mother superior, "but what is your definition of genius?"

I smiled. "Good question," I said. "Very good question. And I'd like you to know that I'm using the definition from Webster's New World American Language Dictionary of pre-1990, which states for genius: 'guardian deity, or spirit of a person; spirit, natural ability, and according to ancient Roman belief, a guardian spirit assigned to a person at birth.' Thank you, Sister, thank you very much.

"And you can now see that originally genius had nothing to do with being smart and/or having a high I.Q., and had everything to do with Spirit." I stopped and breathed so this could sink in. "In fact," I said, "this backs up what my *mamagrande* always told me about coming to this world with a Guardian Angel, and this is why I was raised up with the understanding that I was a genius, that we were all geniuses, because my *mamagrande* also told me that the corn had its own Guardian Angel, the string beans, too, and this was how the corn knew how to grow and what to do and the string beans also knew how to grow and what to do. So now that you can see that originally being a genius had nothing to do with arrogance, I.Q., and/or being smart, how many of you can now say 'I am a genius'?"

Three more nuns raised their hands.

"Good! Good! Excellent!" I said. "And now let me share a little story with you that I think will help all of us get over this hump of being overly educated."

And saying this, I walked back over to the podium and stretched out both arms, gripping the top of the grand old wooden structure and leaned on it as I continued.

"This happened a few years back in Florida when I was giving a talk to about 1,500 teachers and librarians," I said. "And at first, I'll tell you, I was also having to pull teeth to get them to say that they were geniuses, just as I'm having trouble now. But then I saw this young, very good-looking woman in her 30s in the 6th or 7th row to my right and she was crying. She just couldn't say it, and she really wanted to, and seeing this, it suddenly came to me what to do, and I asked the two women beside her to hug her, to give her love, and then once she'd calmed down, I asked this woman if she could please close her eyes and go back to a childhood memory before kindergarten when she'd been happy. She said she could and she closed her eyes, and I then asked her to see herself in a park having fun with her friends, or playing with a puppy, or by the seashore, or wherever, then I asked her if she was there, and she nodded yes. 'Good,' I said to her, 'very good, and now can this happy child say that she's a genius?'"

"Oh, you should have seen it, her whole face lit up with joy and she nodded yes, yes, yes! And so I then said, 'WELL, THEN SAY IT! Say 'I am a genius'. And she did, saying it with Power and Conviction and people applauded and some even had tears in their eyes, and I then had them all say it again and again! And COLLECTIVELY WE THEN EXPLODED! WE TRANSFORMED!

"And so now I want all of you here to STAND UP AND STRETCH! Because, you see, as I said earlier, this is a very emotionally and sensually driven planet, and so you need to feel it! And/or as my dad would always say when he'd have a drink or shake someone's hand, 'You got to feel it!' And so now I need for all of you to give each other a big hug! A big hug full of friendship and Love*Amor*. And yes, this also means you guys in the back. COME ON! IT WON'T HURT! Good! Good! Much better! And now I want all of you to close your eyes and go back to a happy day that you had before you started school. In the park. By the seashore. At a picnic. In the woods. Do you see this day? Just nod. Good! Good! And now that you're into this happy day with feelings of joy, and BIG BIG HAPPINESS! Can that little child within you say, 'I am a genius!'?"

The whole place now EXPLODED, too! And it was beautiful! Almost everyone was saying it, and I now Knew that Henry Miller had been an absolute genius to give me this guidance, because you COULD FEEL IT! Really feel it! All these old retired nuns and priest had LEAPED back into the happiness they'd had as a child! And so now, Collectively, we could move mountains! Tears of joy came to my eyes. WE'D DONE IT! We really had! We'd just traveled those 18 inches from the brain to the Heart*Corazon* and now we were really Hollow bones, Buffalo Bones, Human Being Instruments of God ready to spread His/Her Love*Amor* throughout the UNIVERSE!

"GOOD! GREAT!" I shouted. "And now that you're all once more officially kinder-garden kids, how many of you can imagine World Harmony and Peace and Abundance for All for 5,000 years, even with all the destructive sick crap that's going on globally?"

All the nuns raised their hands and about half of the priests.

"Good! Good! Because, you see, the custom some Native American tribes of Central America have when you meet someone, especially a stranger, is to say, "Finally we meet, for you are another me, and I am another you.' Then they put their hands behind their back and touch their foreheads together."

"Which tribes are these?" asked Mark.

"I don't exactly know," I said, "this was first gifted to me by Mariano, my brother-in-law of my second successful marriage and divorce from his sister Juanita. But I assume that it's a greeting among many tribes. Juanita's mother is from Peru. Okay, now how are all of you feeling?"

"Wonderful!" said one nun, smiling with ecstasy.

"Happy!" said another, with tears of joy.

And so the comments went on and on and then came a statement that stopped all of us.

"I can see them!" said a nun. "I can see our Spirit Guests, and I can see my . . . my own parents."

People were stunned.

"Really?" asked several nuns.

"Oh, yes!" said this nun. "I'm back at that happy day as a child when we were all in the backyard of my grandmother's house and my parents are young and all of us kids have been given white, furry Easter bunnies."

"Real ones?" asked another nun.

"Yes, real rabbits! And their little hearts are beating so fast as we kids hold them and love them."

"We were once given real rabbits for Easter, too," said another nun. "And it was one of the happiest days of my life."

"And you loved to hug those rabbits, didn't you?" I said.

"Oh, yes!" said the nun who was seeing the Spirit World.

"Yes," I said, "because, you see, to reach Spirit we also need to be anchored, and one of the most wonderful ways to feel anchored is to hug, especially when we sleep.

Puppies all sleep rolled up together. Baby ducks and baby chicks cuddle up under their mother's wings."

"Just wait," said a priest to the nun who'd had her breakthrough, "are you telling us that you really see people in these empty chairs and that you just traveled back to your childhood and are with your young parents in your grandmother's backyard?"

"Yes, that's what I'm saying."

"But how can you be at all these places at once?"

"I don't know," said the nun, and we could see it in her face that she was losing sight of her Happy Vision.

I stepped in. "Sister," I said, "please don't try to explain anything to this Doubting Thomas. He's the problem! And he and his type have been the *problema* for the last 13,000 years! And all of you nuns please now hug our Visionary Sister, because, you see, it takes Love and Faith for us to open our HeartEyes and pass through the doors of the Garden of Eden that have opened up for her. Because we never, never, never lost the Holy Garden within, within our own Kingdom of God, and this is where we are all now going to go. No joke! We're on our way! And in the future any of you Doubting Thomases talk to me! Not to the ones who've just made their first breakthrough. But me, who's been going to the Garden through fire and storm for over 40 years and 265 rejections!" I was pissed. I needed a little break. "Okay. Let's take a 10 minute break, and then WE'RE GOING FOR IT! GOD BLESS US ALL!"

And saying this, I walked over and joined the nuns who were hugging our Visionary Sister. Father James came over and so did Mark, and our Love*Amor* Energy was so Powerful, that we just Knew in Our Collective Heart*Corazon*, that we could move MOUNTAINS!

# Seven

I went to my room, washed my face, then I did something I hadn't done in years. Instead of just standing up and talking to God, I knelt alongside my bed, made the sign of the cross over myself, closed my eyes, and thanked the Holy Creator for His/Her Trust and Patience and Guidance and Understanding. And this felt so good that I got lightheaded and had to lie down and I was out like a light.

Then waking up, I felt so happy! BIG BIG HAPPY and ready to go, and looking at the clock on the bed stand, I could see that once more I'd only slept for eight minutes. I laughed. This was utterly amazing! And once again it felt like I'd had a full night's sleep! Then I went dancing down the stairs, and entering the room, I saw that not all of the priests had returned.

"Okay," I said, "I can see that not all of us came back, and that's okay, because now that we're all geniuses, we are going to start geniusing, and so we don't want any negative energy holding us back. Because, you see, once we are geniusing, then all of our *problemas* of the whole world disappear. No joke. They really, really do."

I glanced around and took in a deep breath. "All right, would anyone like to share what happened to them during our little break? Myself, I knelt down and gave thanks to the Almighty and got to feeling so good I became lightheaded and had to lie down, then when I woke up eight minutes later, I felt WONDERFUL! And still feel ABSOLUTELY WONDERFUL!"

A nun raised her hand.

"Yes?" I said.

"Well," she said with a huge smile, "I heard a voice speaking to me in Gaelic. And I haven't heard Gaelic since my family and I visited our relatives in Ireland when I was a young girl."

I smiled. "And how did that feel?"

"Wonderful! Exciting! And the Gaelic language is so beautiful!"

"Yes!" I said. "And there's a reason for that. Because, you see, as Geniuses we are now Jesusing, meaning that we, too, are now Being Directly Guided by God, by our Inner Voice, by our Guardian Angel, and we can now start to see things that we were never able to see before, and this is when we realize that there are no such things as *problemas* here on planet earth, and once we realize this, then a WHOLE NEW UNIVERSE OF POSSIBILITIES OPEN UP FOR US!

"You see," I said, closing my eyes, "problems were deliberately created to siphon off Our Direct Spiritual Energies, so that we are then incapable of ever realizing who we, Human Beings, really are. Do you see what I'm driving at? Problems only exist because of opposing opinions. One group is for abortion, and another is against abortion. One group is saying that there is global warming and another group says there isn't global warming. And each opposing group uses all the facts they can assemble to back up their side of the argument, and the key words they use in European languages are 'the', 'or', and 'but', and these words don't even exist when we start Genius-Jesusing."

"Jesusing?" said a priest.

"Yes," I said, opening my eyes, "because Geniusing is, in fact, Jesusing for we are then Godding. Okay, no more please. Just fasten your seatbelts, because here we go! You see, right after *Rain of Gold* came out with Arte Publico from the University of Houston, I was invited to speak at the National Librarian Conference in Nashville, Tennessee. I was pretty nervous. This was my first big talk in years and I didn't want to blow it like I'd almost done with the English Teachers Conference back at Long Beach when my first book *Macho!* had come out. So I gave my little 15 minute talk about *Rain of Gold,* explaining that this book was so important to me that I'd asked my old mother to please mortgage her home so we could buy the rights back from Putnam in New York, because—I couldn't believe it—they 'd wanted to call if fiction!"

I stopped. I had to take in a big, deep breath before I could go on. "Then I explained to these librarians and teachers that books were Holy, that good books could take people out of their isolated existence and bring them together with Heart and Soul, and this was why every people, every culture needed their own Holy Voice and that *Rain of Gold* was the Holy Voice of my people, just like the Bible was the Holy Voice of the Jews, and Homer was the Holy Voice of the Greeks, and Confucius was the Holy Voice of the Chinese.

"Tears were running down my face by the time I finished my talk, so I went to the bathroom, figuring that I'd blown it and made a fool of myself, but then coming out of the bathroom I saw that most authors had three or four people waiting for them, but one author in the back had everyone in a huge long line waiting for him or her. I asked the tall, well-dressed guy, who'd come out of the bathroom with me, who was that author who had everyone. And he said that it was me. I was shocked. I had no idea what I'd said to cause this, and the place was supposed to close down at 11 p.m., but they had to keep it open until 1 a.m. in the morning, because the librarians and teachers kept demanding to see me. And all this time, as I was signing books and then pamphlets, because we'd run out of books, I'd noticed that there were two Native Americans squatted down over by a corner waiting for me. And after the last person was gone, they both got to their feet and came to me with huge smiles. One guy was real tall and the other was much shorter.

"'You did it, Brother,' said the shorter one. 'YOU KNOCKED THEM DEAD!'

"'Yeah,' agreed the taller one with the huge wide shoulders, 'you really cleaned house!'

"'Yep," said the shorter one, 'you really got to the Whiteman's ear, and that's not an easy task to do.'

"But I didn't understand what they were saying, because I'd just given a little talk about my parents coming to the U.S. with their indigenous mothers from Mexico. And I knew it was a good story, but so were the stories of these other writers. This was when the shorter one introduced himself, saying that he was Harry Walters from Arizona, and he was Navajo. Then the big one said he was Jack Big Shoulders from Montana and he was Lakota, then he teased how all the white women just couldn't stop kissing me and hugging me. And it was true. I must've gotten 500 kisses that night, but I still couldn't understand why my talk had touched these people so deeply.

"You gave them Hope!" said the Navajo.

"You gave them Spirit!" said the Lakota.

"'Yes,' I'd said, 'but some of these other speakers were really good and had great stories filled with hope and spirit, too, and yet they hardly got anyone to come to their booths. So, why me?'

"I remember that the Navajo and the Lakota now looked at each other, and Harry said, 'Then you really don't understand what it is you did tonight?'

"I nodded, and this was when Jack Big Shoulders said, 'Brother, you just turned all of history on its ear, and you opened up doors the Whiteman has never seen open before, or at least not for the last 7,000 years!'

"'Exactly,' said Harry, 'you brought our native way of thinking and viewing the world right up in their faces and touched their hearts as they've never been touched.'

"'Look,' said the tall Lakota, 'the westward movement is over. They have no more continents to conquer, no more people to annihilate or enslave, and you just gave them a whole new world of possibilities!'

"'You see,' said the Navajo. 'when you said that every day is another miracle gifted to us by God, and that your Native American grandmothers taught you to give greetings every morning to Father Sun, the Right Eye of God, and to watch Our Sister Corn smile her happy face and Our Sister Flowers open up with joy and Our Brother Birds begin to sing with Love *Amor*, you were giving Hope and Spirit and a Nature Love that touched their Hearts, and then when you said that the Mother Moon was the Left Eye of God and that the Stars were our Holy Family, because we, too, were Walking Stars, you tied it all together, because you then added that we, Human People, also had Our Holy Sacred Work to do here on Mother Earth, just like Our Sister Corn and Brother String Beans.'

"'In other words, you were giving the Whiteman back his Original Instructions,' the big Lakota told me, and he then explained to me that Whiteman had been lost for a very long time, and that they now didn't know where else to go or what to do, and I'd just given meaning to their lives by maybe returning to their own Indigenous Roots.

"'You showed them,' he said, 'in a way that they could understand, that their ancestors weren't savages, but in fact, were intelligent, well-thought-out, good people who'd lived in a sustainable way with nature.'

"'I did all that?' I'd said to them. 'But I just talked for 15 minutes about my family.'

"Hearing this, they both laughed and laughed, and then they began to speak in Navajo or maybe in the Lakota language. I couldn't understand a single word they said, yet I kind of remembered, like in a dream, some of these throaty sounds and the use of tongue clicks that, I guess, I'd heard as a child from my Yaqui *mamagrande* and my uncle Archie, who had relatives out at the Pala reservation in California. Then the two of them stopped talking to each other and turned back to me.

"'You tell him,' said the Navajo to the Lakota.

"'No, you tell it to him, Brother,' the Lakota said to the Navajo.

"'Okay,' replied Harry Walters, looking at me. 'We both believe that maybe you don't really understand what it is that you said tonight. And it's important that you do, because obviously you will be speaking again, because you have reached the Whiteman's ear.'

"'Exactly,' said the Lakota. 'You got the Whiteman's attention, and that's a very difficult thing to do, Brother.'

"'You know,' I said, 'over and over my parents would tell me that I really didn't understand what it was they were telling me. My dad, in fact, finally said that I was *tapado,* meaning constipated in my head.'

"They both busted out laughing.

"'Your dad told it true,' said Jack Big Shoulders.

"'Thanks,' I replied.

"'Let me try to explain to you what I think it was that your parents were trying to tell you,' said Harry.

"'Go ahead,' I said, glancing at the tall, muscular Lakota. He was all smiles.

"'In the Navajo languaging,' continued Harry Walters, 'and in every native languaging that I know of, there is no concept of nouns. All there are is verbs.'

"'So,' I wondered, 'what's that got to do with anything?'

"Hearing this, the Lakota burst out laughing again.

"'Everything,' said the Navajo.

"'But how can that be?' I asked. 'A tree—that's a noun. It can't be a verb.'

"'Sure it can, because a tree is alive and always growing and changing through the seasons and through the years. It's *tree-ing,* a verb.'

"I gripped my forehead. "'Okay, but what about rocks? They don't change.'

"'Yes, they do. If we lived to be ten million years old, we'd see that they are constantly changing, too.'

"'Oh, God, this is really confusing,' I said. 'But, well, didn't Einstein say that all there is, is change?'

"'Yes, he did, so he was doing it the Navajo way, just like you did it the Navajo way tonight.'

"'No, the Lakota way!' said the big man from Montana, still laughing.

"'All right,' I said, trying to figure out what they were saying, 'if everything is a verb, then do you believe in God?'

"'No, of course not,' said the Navajo, without batting an eye. 'That would be silly. We *do* God.'

"'You *do* God?' I said, gripping my forehead with both hands. Having been raised a Catholic, this was just so confusing that it hurt my head. 'But how in the world can you do God?'" I asked. 'Hell—I mean, Heaven—we can't even agree on the concept of Who or what God is.

"'That's the whole point,' said the Lakota.

"'What's the point?'

"'Why native people have kept the Creator as a verb.'

"'Dammit,' I said, 'talk plain! You guys are killing me in my head!'

"'Years of constipation will have that effect on a man when he's finally trying to take a good mental shit,' said the Lakota, roaring with laughter.

"But I didn't laugh. I was in terrible pain!

"'When we walk in Beauty, we are doing God,' continued Harry. 'When we are in Harmony with our surroundings, we are part of God. And when we find Peace within us, we are God.'

"'YOU ARE GOD!?!' I shouted. 'No wonder the *padres* tried to slaughter all you savages! I mean, all of us savages! How in the hell—I mean, in Heaven—can we, human beings, be God?'

"'Easy. We are God as a verb, not as a noun. We are Goding once we find Peace inside of us,' the Navajo told me

"'GODING!' I shouted with my whole head EXPLODING! I had to sit down. And the damn Lakota wouldn't stop laughing.

"'Dammit,' I finally said, 'I still don't get it! Goding? Goding? Are you then saying that it doesn't really matter what you think, and it only matters what you do?'

"'Now you're beginning to get it,' said the Lakota.

"'Well, if this is true, then it really doesn't matter if you are a Catholic, a . . . a Protestant, a Jew, a Muslim, a Buddhist, a born-again Christian, or even an atheist, because all that really matters is what you do, right? Not what you think or believe.'

"'Exactly!' said the Lakota.

"'Then we would have never, ever had any religious wars,' I said.

"'NOW YOU HAVE IT, BROTHER!' shouted the Lakota.

"'Then we've had all of our religious wars, not because of religion, but because of the language we use to do our talking and thinking about our religions.'

"'Now you really got it, Brother!' said the Navajo.

"'This is mind-boggling! It changes all of history!' I said.

"'And this is exactly what you did tonight,' explained Harry. 'You changed the course of history!'

"'But how did I do this?' I asked.

"'You did it tonight,' replied the Navajo, 'when you said that your two Native American grandmothers didn't believe in God; they *lived* with God. You did it tonight when you said that your grandmothers didn't pray to God; they *spoke* to God. You did it tonight when you said God was their way of life, and you did it when you said that we're all Walking Stars and we came to Mother Earth with a Guardian Angel to plant the Stardust Seeds that we brought with us from the Heavens, and that God needed us as much as we needed God in order to plant His ongoing Sacred Garden. You totally changed the course of human history, because God was no longer unreachable and perfect, but instead close and very reachable.'

"I was stunned! They were right! I had said all this!

"'Yes, Brother, you had them eating out of your hand,' added the Lakota, 'and they were all ready to follow you anywhere, because in making God both male and female, you rolled back human history 13,000 years to the last ice age.'

"And I can tell you that those two guys kept talking to me, explaining my own book *Rain of Gold* to me, but I'd quit listening. I'd had it. They walked me to the elevator. They were staying across the way, where the rooms were more reasonable. The only reason I was staying at the hotel of the convention center was because my room had been paid for by the library association. And the big man from Montana was still talking, and I guess telling me something really important, but I just couldn't take it in. I was dead on my feet and I almost collapsed once I got into the elevator. And then that night I had a flying dream and I was with my dad, shooting across the Heavens and this was when I realized that our Mother Earth really was no larger than a grain of sand on the Seashore of Creation and we, Human Beings, were so huge that our arms and legs reach out to the furthest reaches of the Universe, because God was a Verb and we were Verbs, too. Supreme Being was God and Human Beings were we. Both Verbs.

"Okay," I now said, "all that happened to me in Nashville, Tennessee, but it really didn't register what all this verb stuff meant until about a month later when I was at the wrong hotel about 80 miles outside of Phoenix, Arizona, and the next morning I was scheduled to do a TV interview at 7 a.m. But there are no accidents, because being at this wrong hotel with the Heavens jam-packed full of Stars was when it hit me with SUCH POWER what that Navajo and Lakota had been telling me as I'd gotten into the elevator that I went two years without sleeping! No joke! Just like Albert Einstein, I, too, became a Beam of Light!

"Ready? Because I now have a question for you Genius-Jesusing people that will also BURST YOU INTO BEING BEAMS OF LIGHT! Ready? Good. Good. And now close your eyes, and when you see the answer within your own Kingdom of God, I want you to raise up your hand, but please don't give the answer aloud.

"No, we need for over 50% of you to get this answer on your own, before we say it aloud. Because, like I said, when I realized the answer to this question I'm going to ask you, an Energy came BURSTING into me with such power that I really, really went two years without sleeping. And I then understood how my Great Great Great Great Great Aunt, Mother Of No Specific Child, had gotten to the age of 165 and how she could've gone on to the age 900 years, like Moses, in perfect health, because we, Human People, are, in fact, Living, Breathing Beams of Light! Okay, ready? Here is the question, but please just raise your hand. We need over 50% of you to get it on your own," I said, wetting my lips that had gone dry. "When did Creation happen if . . . if everything is a Verb?"

No one raised their hand.

"Come on," I said, "trees are tree-ing, rocks are rocking, and Albert Einstein proved that all there is is change."

One hand shot up. Then another and another. All three nuns.

"Good," I said. "We have three people who see it, and now I want you three to put your hands down and send your Love*Amor* to all the rest of our people, and I want you others to close your eyes and breathe in the Love*Amor* that is Being sent to you, because we're All, All, All Interconnected, we're All, All, All Interplanetary Connected to the furthest reaches of the UNIVERSE! Good! Good!"

And this was when the priests who hadn't returned to our session now came quickly walking in and took their seats. One was a very big bulldog-looking guy. I guess that they'd been in the next room listening.

I laughed. "All right, and you guys who just came in, you, too, close your eyes, and breathe in deeply, and I ask all of you once again, when did Creation happen if everything is a Verb? Trees are tree-ing, rocks are rocking, and Einstein proved that all there is is change. NOW GO FOR IT within your own Kingdom of God and raise your hands!"

Two more hands came up, but not with as much confidence as the first three.

"All right," I said, "now everyone open your eyes, and get up and stretch. We have about 25%, and what we need to happen is for all of us together to Circulate the Love*Amor* Energy that's shooting around us, so stretch! Stretch! And breathe deeply, then blow out fast! Yes! Yes! And do it a few more times. Good! Good! And now please take your seats again."

They did so.

"Great!" I said. "And so now tell me, when did Creation happen if everything is a Verb?"

Six more hands shot up, and these came up with energy and confidence.

'WONDERFUL!" I shouted. "WE DID IT! We got well over 50%! So tell it! Speak it! Verbalize it! When did Creation happen if everything is a Verb?"

"RIGHT NOW!" shouted one of the nuns who'd first raised her hand.

"ALWAYS!" shouted another nun who'd also been one of the first to raise her hand.

"It's still happening!" said a priest.

"It has never ceased happening!" said another priest.

"It's ongoing forever!"

"YES! YES!" I shouted. "You're all right. So you see, we didn't get left out of the Super Bowl! And that guy in the wheelchair doesn't get it, because he's stuck in nouns and in five senses, because there are no beginnings and ends! IT'S STILL BANGING! Right Here! Right Now! Forever! So how does this feel?"

"I think it's mind boggling," said a priest.

"Well, then, stop thinking. Because all thinking is done with manmade words and manmade words are limiting within their own definition, and so we need to get into our feelings, are Knowingness, which is INFINITE! So I ask again, how does this FEEL?"

"Look," said the same priest, "this is still too new for me to think about it."

I laughed. "So stop thinking! You see, what happened is that nouns are one of the things that we ate from the Tree of Knowledge, and with nouns we solidified creation, and then we imposed our manmade concept on Creation. We said, this empire started here and ended there. This king started ruling here and his ruling ended here. And we then took our idea of beginnings and endings and imposed them on nature. So can you now begin to see, to feel, to glimpse that the doors of the Garden of Eden are re-opening? Eh, can you glimpse this?"

All the nuns nodded and several of the priests nodded, too.

"Good, good," I said, "and now that you can clearly begin to see that Creation is ongoing, tell me what happened to the old concept of death? Go ahead. Talk it, speak it, put it in words right now!"

"It . . . it disappears," said a nun, with her eyes getting huge.

"It never existed," said another nun in astonishment.

"Then we're always dying and living," said a priest.

"I read somewhere that every seven years all the cells of our bodies renew, so that infers that the old ones died," said *Margarita*.

"Oh, my Lord God," said another nun, "then this is what you were referring to when you said that once we Activate the Kingdom of God within us, we begin Living on the Active Side of Eternity!"

I nodded. "Yes, exactly," I said, with tears of joy were streaming down my face. "And now that we have slipped out of the two old concepts of nouns and death that have been holding us back, and we see that Genius-Jesusing and Creation have always been ongoing, now I'd like to ask you who . . . who are we in Full Partnership with?"

"WITH GOD!" shouted a nun.

"With Creation!" said another nun.

"And so we now no longer believe in God, but live with God," said another nun, "just as your grandmothers were living with Our Holy Creator."

"Exactly," I said. "And so how does this feel?"

"FANTASTIC!" screamed a nun, leaping to her feet.

"WONDERFUL!" yelled another nun.

"For the first time in my life I can love God without fear," said another nun with tears running down her face.

"Can't talk," said *Margarita*. "Too beautiful! Too beautiful!" And she also had tears of joy running down her beautiful, elegant face.

"WE NEED TO TELL THE POPE!" shouted a priest from the back. "This could revolutionize the whole Church!"

"DIDN'T YOU HEAR HIM?" yelled Mary. "The Pope is a man! And over and over he's told us that it's now women who are going to lead! And men need to listen and 'follow in front'!"

"Well, yes, but it can help," said the priest, sounding defensive.

"How can it help?" said the nun. "What we need is a woman Pope!"

"A woman Pope?" said several priests at the same time.

I raised up my hand. "Please," I said, "understand that what we can imagine, then voice aloud, becomes our reality, and so yes, yes, yes, we are very quickly going to have a woman Pope, and . . . and the Vatican will be moved from Italy to Ireland."

"YES, THAT'S IT!" shouted a nun. "This was what I heard the Voice telling me in Gaelic, but it was so fantastic sounding that I didn't think that I'd heard correctly."

"You heard correctly," I said, wiping the tears out of my eyes, "and after the Vatican has been in Ireland for 100 years, using the Native language of Gaelic instead of the dead, non-changing language of Latin, the Vatican will then go to Mexico for 100 years and take on a non-empire-based Native Language for a 100 years, then go to the Philippines for a 100 years and take on another Native languaging, and then come back to Europe at a rich valley between France and Germany and take on the pre-Roman Native languaging of the Druids for 100 years, then shoot down to Africa, zigzagging from Africa and the Americas and Asia and all around the world every 100 years for the next 52,000 years, becoming truly catholic—"

"AND CATHOLIC MEANS UNIVERSAL!" shouted the big burly bulldog-looking priest.

"Yes," I said, "that's what we Catholics are always told. But have you ever looked up the word 'catholic' in the dictionary?"

He shook his head.

"Well, Father—"

"Joe," he said, "just call me Joe."

"Well, Joe, I suggest that you look up the word 'catholic' and you'll find that the definition doesn't end with 'universal'. No, the full definition, according to the pre-1990 Webster American Language Dictionary is 'universal, all inclusive, of general interest and value, having broad sympathies and understanding; hence, liberal'."

They were stunned.

"Yes, I, too, was shocked," I said, "when I looked up the word 'catholic', and . . . and now I'd like for you to consider what Bishop Malachy from Ireland said in the 11th century."

"He said that we'd have 113 Popes," said Joe.

"And our next Pope will be number 113, and he'll be from the Americas and a Jesuit, just like my brilliant *amigo* Greg from Chicago, and he'll set us up for Our First Official Woman Pope just as Jesus let me Know when he gifted me His Holy Sacred Heart*Corazon* in Madrid, Spain back in 1992. And . . . and all of you already KNOW ALL THIS DEEP WITHIN OUR COLLECTIVE CELLULAR MEMORY!"

I stopped.

I took in a deep breath and blew it out fast. They were all staring at me, so I closed my eyes and just kept breathing in deeply and blowing out fast.

"HOGWASH!" yelled Joe. "Bishop Malachy wasn't correct about everything, you know!"

"It's not hogwash!" snapped Mary. "Since everything is a Verb and we are then all in Full Partnership with God, how can we then not Know this to Be True within our own Kingdom of God!"

This was a brilliant answer, but I could also see it wasn't quite satisfying Joe and the other priests.

"Joe, I suggest that you just go back to that place within you," said *Margarita,* "when he asked us to consider how we'd all be today if Peter would have not looked down, and he would have walked on water alongside Our Lord Jesus. And I then do believe that you won't even be arguing with Mr. Villaseñor."

"Yes, she's right!" said another nun. "And you priests didn't help raise the money to have Mr. Villaseñor come to see us, so I say, SHUT UP! Or please leave so we can continue this Enlightening Event! A woman Pope," she added, with tears of joy coming to her eyes. "It makes Total Sense, especially since we are finishing up 26,000 years of male energy and going into 26,000 years of female energy!"

Two priests got to their feet, looking all upset, I guess for being told to shut up by a nun.

"OH, SIT DOWN!" shouted Mary. "You guys are too old to revolt, and besides, it's us, the nuns, who fix your food and do your laundry, so just get off your high and mighty crap, and sit back down!"

The two old priests sat back down, and some of the nuns started laughing with so much fun and *gusto* that I couldn't help it, and I started laughing, too.

# Eight

We broke for dinner and I went into the large bathroom just off the main dining room where we were scheduled to dine in the evening. It was a huge, ornate beautiful bathroom and I'd just unzipped and was starting to take a pee, when the door suddenly opened behind me with a bang and there stood Joe, the big burly priest and his face was all red with rage.

"MY GOD!" he shouted. "YOU JUST DON'T STOP!"

"Excuse me," I said, "but I'm trying to pee!"

"SO PISS! NO ONE'S HOLDING YOU BACK!"

And saying this, he turned and closed the bathroom door, locking it, and then came walking towards me. I suddenly didn't need to pee anymore. This huge man outweighed me by a good 80 pounds and it didn't look like he carried much fat, so even with all my knowledge of having been a wrestler and having been trained in advanced boot camp in the Army, I figured that I really had very little chance to defend myself against this huge guy in such close quarters.

"I need to speak with you!" he said, gasping for air.

"Well, okay, good," I said, "but could we do it outside on the grass by the lake after I pee?"

"NO!" he shouted. "This needs to be private! Pee! I'll wait!"

"In here with me?"

"YES!"

"Well, okay, but I don't think I can pee with you watching," I said.

"All right, then you can pee afterward, and I'll just tell you what I need to tell you right now," he said.

"Okay," I said, glancing around to see if there was any chance of escape.

"I'm a cross dresser!" he said.

"You're a what?" I said.

"You heard me, A CROSS DRESSER, DAMNIT!"

"Okay," I said, "but, well, you see, I need a little help. I don't exactly know what that means. Are you telling me that you're gay?"

"NO, I'M NOT GAY!" he barked. "I'm straight! This has nothing to do with being gay! You see, I was raised by my mother, a big woman, and I'd see her put on her make up and get all dolled up to go to bars to find a man for the night, and well, it angered me that I wasn't enough for my mom, but then once, when she was gone, I sat down before her mirror and I began putting on makeup like I'd been watching her do for years, and it calmed me down, especially when I looked at myself in the mirror and saw an attractive young woman. So, well, after that, I then began doing it every time she went out, and I became a big kid, so by 14 I was able to fill out her dresses, and this was when she once brought home this man who was abusive to her, I . . . I, well, literally BEAT THE LIVING SHIT OUT OF HIM and threw him out, and I guess she thought I was one of her girlfriends, so she thanked me and then in the morning she thought it had all been a dream."

"So then, you were dressed like a woman when you beat the crap out of that man and threw him out?" I asked.

"YES! OF COURSE! THAT'S THE WHOLE POINT! As a man I've never beat the hell out of anyone, but dressed like a woman, I've . . . I've, well, brought many situations to justice, and then when I became a chaplain attached to the U.S. Marines and some of our G.I.s would confess to me the horrible things they'd do, not just in war, but at home with their own families, I'd go to my place afterwards and put on makeup and get all dolled up and, forgive me God, but dressed as a woman I would go find these Marines and I'd beat the living crap out of them, and THEN I COULD FORGIVE THEM!" he yelled and then took in a huge deep breath and blew out fast. "Do you now see what I'm talking about? As a woman I can forgive, BUT NOT AS A MAN!"

It was me who now took in a great big deep breath. I had absolutely no idea how to respond to this, and here I'd figured that this great big tough-looking guy had probably abused altar boys and maybe even other priests. Never had it crossed my mind that he'd dressed up like a woman and defended women. Then I laughed. I mean, he'd had to have looked pretty attractive to have lured those Marines in so close.

"You're pretty big," I said, laughing. "So it must've been pretty difficult to find attractive dresses large enough to fit you!"

He started laughing, too. "It was," he said, "so I had to learn how to make alterations."

"And only as a woman have you beat the crap out of men?"

"Yes, that's true," he said. "Only as a woman, and this is why I had to see you privately."

"But not to beat me, right?" I said. "Because you're dressed like a man."

"Oh, no," he said, "I came to tell you how wonderful it is to hear all the things that you're telling us, because then, maybe, I'm . . . I'm not going to go to hell and burn for eternity when I die," he said with tears suddenly coming to his eyes. "Because revenge and not forgiveness I can now see is what I did for most of my life as, well, supposedly, a man of God."

I took in another great big deep breath and blew out fast. My God, my God, my God, then this big tough-looking man had truly been paying attention to all I'd said.

"You know," I said, "I can now see that you were really taking in all that I've been talking about, and here I'd thought you were really just being sarcastic."

"Oh, no, not at all," he said. "It's quite the opposite. I . . . I, well, saw you levitate."

"Leva-what?"

"Levitate, rise up off the floor."

"You saw me do that?" I said, swallowing. This frightened me. Only once before had anyone ever said that they'd seen me do this.

"Yes, when you repeated the words 'I am a genius' over and over again, then you made the connection that Geniusing was, in fact, Jesusing, at that point you levitated and Prince saw it, too."

"Prince?"

"Yes, that's what we call Father James, because he was the chaplain in Washington, D.C. and all those high and mighty came to confess to him. He and Margaret both saw you levitate. You're not alone, Mr. Villaseñor," he added. "Some of us have had experiences that aren't too much different than your own."

Once more I took in a deep breath, and I flashed on the Archangel I'd met in Chicago, then I flashed on the L.A. rush hour traffic parting for me like the Red Sea, then I flashed on the realization that I really wasn't alone and so none of these Miracles and even Levitating were really me. No, they were simply proof that we were All, All, All Interconnected with Creation Creating, and that there were others all over our planet who were also already coming forward and stepping up to the plate in preparation for this shift that would happen on December 21, 2012, so Collectively we could help plant Our Stardust Seeds in profusion until November 10, 2026 at 3pm California time.

"Okay," I said to him, "I think I can piss now."

"Do you want me to leave?" he asked.

"No, you might as well stay," I said. "My God, a cross dresser and a Chaplain attached to the Marines. Wow! What a life you've lived!"

"That's not all of it," he said.

I turned my back on him, unzipped again, and began to pee.

"You should talk to Prince," he said. "He's the one who's really had the life, hearing the confessions of all those movers and shakers in Washington D.C. Those confessions make the atrocities that I heard from our fighting boys sound like child's play. You're dad was right, our whole damn world really is upside down and stupid, and don't you think for a minute that the Church isn't still asking us to sprinkle holy water on the atrocities that She allows our good Christian soldiers to commit, and then has us say the equivalent to these service men that they only killed their earthly bodies, but they saved their immortal souls for the love of God and the honor of the United States.

"And these young men believe us, because we're priests, and I used to believe it, too, until now that I've been retired, and for these last 15 years I've had a chance to reflect. Truly, I now believe that more of us of the cloth are going to go to hell when we die than regular people, because we out-Nixoned Nixon. Watergate was nothing compared to what we've been hiding for centuries."

"And yet you were still able to see me levitate," I said. "And I've only had one other person ever tell me that she saw me levitate. It was a woman healer from Carlsbad who self-published a book about healing yourself."

"Carlsbad, New Mexico?"

"No, Carlsbad, California, and as I'm sure you know, only a very Spiritually Elevated Human Soul can see levitation, so I'm sure that you're not going to hell," I added.

"How can I not be? Judgment Day is just around the corner and that's the Day when Jesus is returning to—"

"No," I said, "it's not coming."

"Judgment Day isn't coming?" he asked.

"No, it's already here. And Judgment Day is the day when we all stop passing judgment on each other, and especially on ourselves."

He looked all confused.

"Didn't Jesus say to forgive them for they did not know?" I said.

"Well, yes, He did, but—"

"There are no 'buts' in life," I said, "because you're also part of the package that doesn't know. Stop being so full of self-importance that you think that you're superior to those who drove the nails into Our Lord Jesus' flesh. You are every bit as ignorant as they were. In fact, if Jesus were to come to us right now, today, who do you think would be the first ones to want to do him in?"

"I don't know," he said.

"Come on," I said, pissing. "You know. Tell me who's all full of judgment."

"Well, I guess you're pointing at my fellow Christians," he said.

"Exactly," I said. "It is us, you and me and all our most conservative and self-righteous Christians, who'd drive the first nails into Our Lord Jesus if He was to come to us once again."

"Unless He came dressed in fire and damnation!" he added, laughing. "Yeah, I guess you're right. Then you really do think that I'm part of those who didn't know, and so I can be forgiven?"

"Absolutely," I said, "because once we truly open our eyes to the full Glory of God, then we can only do the Sacred Holy Good, and your eyes are just beginning to open now that you're retired and have had time to reflect."

"Then I really am forgivable," he said, with tears coming to his eyes.

"Yes, of course," I said, taking in another deep breath. "You are a good man, Joe. A very good man, and I bet you make a pretty good-looking big girl, too," I added, laughing.

He burst out laughing, too. "It's true," he said. "I watched my mother put on her makeup for all those years and get all dolled up and I'd see this large pretty homely looking woman, totally transform. So you're right, I must say, I did look pretty snazzy when I was young and I'd get myself all dolled up."

I walked across the room and washed my hands after I'd finished pissing. "Has anyone ever seen you?"

"You mean dressed as a woman?"

"Yes."

He became as embarrassed as a little girl. "Prince. He saw me once. But no one else."

"What is it about Prince?" I asked, drying my hands. "It seems like a lot of people entrust him with their darkest—no, not darkest, but their most exciting secrets!"

He yelped. "That's it! That's it! It's because he, too, manages to do what you just did. We tell him our darkest secret, and he gives our secret back to us in Light and Joy, and we then feel totally better about ourselves, and this was what he did with those big-shot movers and shakers in Washington. They all adored him!"

"Yes, and Father James is able to do this, because he's an Archangel," I said.

"Prince is an Archangel?"

"Yes."

"You know, that makes sense," said Joe. "And he's the one who convinced us priests that it was okay for the Sisters to invite you to come and see us."

I nodded, then said, "Okay, and I now need to know how you'd like for us to go out of this bathroom. Do I go out first and you stay here for a couple of minutes, or do we just say to hell with it and go out together arm in arm?"

He looked at me. "You're right," he said, "this is a delicate situation, so, well, maybe we shouldn't go out together," he added. "But I also saw that you didn't have any trouble hugging and kissing Margaret."

"Hey, do I detect a little jealousy?" I said, smiling.

"You're damn right!" he said. "I've been in love with that woman for over 60 years, and I've never so much as held her hand, and here you were hugging her and then kissing her. And Sister Mary, too!"

"You've been in love with *Margarita* for over 60 years?"

"Yes, of course! I'm a priest, but also I'm a man!" he said. "And she's the most beautiful and wonderful woman I've ever met!"

"Well, then why haven't you hugged and kissed her?" I asked.

He broke down crying.

"Is it because you're a priest?" I said. "You know, there are priests who have fallen in love and left the priesthood."

"Yes, of course, I know," he said. "And I've considered that, but then I have to admit to myself that being a priest isn't really what has held me back. What has held me back is that I don't even know how to talk to a woman, and especially not about such feelings like love. And yet I've tried, but then I get all nervous. I'm 85 years old, and—"

"You're 85!" I said. "Hell, I'd thought you were in your late 60s or early 70s!"

"No, I'm 85, and I've never been with a . . . a woman or a man. Sometimes I think these gay priests have it made. They get to have an intimacy I've never experienced."

I had to take in several deep breaths. Wow! Never in 100 million years had I ever expected any of this.

"May I hug you?" I said.

"I thought you'd never ask," he said, opening up his arms and coming to me, and it was a good thing that I'm strong and in great shape, because the bear-like hug he got me in could've broken ribs.

And so we held each other for a long time, and then I finally pulled away.

"Hey, but you kissed her!" he said. "We all saw you kissing Margaret!"

"Okay, okay," I said. "I'll kiss you, too."

And so I kissed him on the right cheek and then the left cheek.

"My dad never even kissed me," he said, wiping tears out of his eyes. "Thank you. I'm in my 80s and this is my first real hug and kiss!"

"Wow!" I said.

And so we looked at each other one last time, smiled, and then we turned and just went out of the bathroom together arm in arm, laughing with *carcajadas*.

"You know, Joe," I said to him once we were walking down the hallway, "when I was hugging *Margarita*, she told me that she hadn't been hugged by a man since her dad last hugged her when she'd been 18 years old, and she's now 91."

He took in a big deep breath. "Then you think," he said, "that she'd be open for me to take her hand and ask her for a hug?"

"Absolutely!" I said. "You're a big strong handsome-looking man."

"Really?"

"Yes, and you don't need to get dolled up," I added.

"Hey, that's confidential! Please, not one word!"

People looked at us as we walked down the hallway, but it seemed like they really didn't care and/or even made the connection that we'd just come out of the bathroom together. They were just happy to see us happy.

I was thirsty. I decided to get a glass of water, and then drink some wine before dinner. Wow! This encounter with Joe had just TOTALLY BLOWN ME AWAY!

# Nine

"All right," I said, "we've just had a wonderful, relaxing dinner, and so I'd like for us to keep this good relaxing feeling before we turn in for the night." I breathed and as usual, it caused most of them to breathe along with me. "And I'm very proud of us," I continued, "for having gotten as far as we have. This is all major stuff. Myself, it's taken me years and years to truly comprehend these things I've shared with you today, and many of you, well, got it so quickly."

A priest raised his hand. We were still in the dining room, sitting at our different tables and sipping coffee, but I didn't drink coffee. If I did, it would keep me up all night.

"Yes," I said.

"Did you really mean it when you said that you went two years without sleeping?"

"Yes, I really meant that."

"But that seems totally impossible! You must have slept!" he added.

"Ask your guides, ask your Guardian Angel tonight to help you with this, and then tell us all about it tomorrow. Because I agree with you, it does seem totally impossible, but walking off a cliff seemed impossible, too, and parting L.A. rush hour traffic, and yet all those are true, too."

"And not just a dream?" he asked.

I took in a deep breath. How could I handle this, because all of Living Life, *la Vida,* was a DreamVoyage. Then it hit me.

"Look," I said, "I wasn't going to get into this tonight, and yet I now believe—I mean, feel and I'm being told that I should get into this right now. You see, in Oaxaca, Mexico before the European people came, it was recognized that there were three centers, not one, for processing information. One center is the Brain Computer and it has 4 Senses, all located at the head: sight, hearing, smelling, and tasting. Specific information from specific location. Another center is the Heart Computer and it has 3 Senses: feeling, balance, and intuition, and these three are done with the whole body. We feel 26 arms-length in all directions. Have you ever walked into a room and immediately felt something was wrong? Of course. We all have. What you did was feel 26 arms-length in all directions with your whole body, and if it all felt balanced, then everything was okay. But if something was out of balance, you instinctively, intuitively, you knew something was wrong.

"And . . . and you knew this with a capital 'K'. You didn't think this. You Knew this and Knowing is 100s of 1000s of years old, whereas our thinking with manmade words is only, at best, maybe 40,000 years old. So thinking is to the Brain Center as intuition and/or the Voice of Genius is to the Heart Center. All right, got that? Good. Good. And now we can move into our third center for processing information, and this is the Soul Center, here in our gut, and this one has 6 Senses. The first of these is Music, the 8th Sense, because when God Created the Universe, He/She Created One United Verse, One United Song, and each of us comes into manifestation with our own Song, and then once we move into this computer, then Time and Space, our 9th and 10$^{th}$ Senses, are relative, as Einstein said, and/or they simply disappear, and we now move into our 11$^{th}$ Sense, which is our Collective Consciousness of All the Past and of All the Future, and we now have—"

"Psychic powers like Bishop Malachy of Ireland!" said the priest who'd said this was all impossible."

"Exactly!" I said. "Because Psychic is to the Soul as Intuition is to the Heart and Thinking is to the Brain!"

"Oh, wow! Then not sleeping for two years is possible!"

"Exactly!" I said. "Because we become Beams of Light just like Albert Einstein, and Light needs no sleep, and it doesn't age, either."

"I see, I see," said the priest, "then everything you've been sharing with us all day is the norm once we Activate our Kingdom of God with our 13 Senses. But what is the 13$^{th}$ Sense?"

"Being," I said. "Supreme Being and Human Being, and this is when we are at one with Goding."

"It's making sense now!" he said. "This is wonderful! And so when I go to sleep tonight, and I stop all of my thinking with manmade words, I'll then be, through feelings, in Direct Communications with God!"

"Exactly," I said. "And now that most of you here are 78 and/or older, please ask tonight for your Blessed Tools with which to become a Sacred Elder. This is one of the main things we're missing in our whole western civilization. We worship youth," I added. "And I love that I'm getting old!"

"ME, TOO!" yelled Joe.

"Anymore questions?" I asked.

"Yes," said a nun. "Why did you refer to the word 'the' so many times?"

"Oh, wow!" I said, taking in a deep breath. "This is a big one. You see, the word 'the' only exists in European-based languages. The Russian language doesn't have it. No Asian language has it. No Indigenous language has it. Only Europe, and it was invented by the Jews and their cousins, and then popularized by the Greeks, and then all of Europe adopted it. And I'm not bad-mouthing the Jews or the Greeks. My ex-wife is Jewish. My two boys are Jewish. And I'm Jewish through digestion. And at first the word 'the' is innocent sounding, because you use it to say 'the tree' in front of my house.

"And the rest of the world has 'that tree' and 'this tree' to show location. Only Europe has 'the tree', but then European people jump from 'the tree' to 'the truth' and what happens to truth? Go on, tell me what happens to truth when you place 'the' in front of it? Come on, you're all geniuses."

No one said a word. They all just looked at each other, and then finally one nun spoke.

"It becomes singular," she said.

"Okay, good, and what else does it do?" I asked.

"It, well, in a way elevates truth," said a priest.

"Okay, excellent, and what else does it do?" I asked again.

People shook their heads.

"Come on," I said, "go for it! What does it do to all other truths?"

"It voids them," said Joe.

"Yes, it voids them, and what else happens?" I asked.

"The truth becomes absolute and there can be no other truths," said Mark.

"*Exactamente!*" I said. "And then how do the words 'or' and 'but' back up 'the truth' Eh, what does 'or' do?"

"It gives us choice," said a priest.

"Does it really?" I asked.

"It limits us into only two choices in respect to 'the'," said Mark.

"*Exactamente!*" I said. "So if I have a third or fourth opinion, I can't voice it because I've been forced into polarity of mind. I either get it or I don't. I agree or I don't. And because you have 'the truth', then I am totally intimidated and so I fold up. And if I don't fold and do speak up, you now use the word 'but' with one 't' and what have you done?"

"I've cancelled out everything you've just said," said Mark.

"Exactly," I said, "and this is why 'the', 'or', and 'but' are by far the . . . the most dangerous words in all the world, and have allowed Europe to take over the globe, and it's not because European people are smarter than others! Oh, no, it's that the language they speak gives them a manipulation and arrogance with the one-and-only absolute truth and then nobody else's truths matter. And then hook up 'the truth' to God and/or politics, and you have a culture that respects no other cultures and that's why in Mexico my great-grandfather Leonardis Camargo slaughtered whole Yaqui Indian villages, women and children, too, and he had no regrets, because he had 'the truth' in the name of Jesus Christ."

Tears came to my eyes. "And my great-grandfather wasn't a bad man. He was a good man. It's just that he didn't know any better because language makes us who we are. We talk with language, we think with language, or process all of our feelings through language. So language makes us who we are and our reality what it is. For instance, I now ask you, what happens to the Bible when you take 'the' away and instead put 'a' in front of Bible?"

I stopped and breathed. You could hear a pin drop.

"Our Bible becomes one of many," said a priest.

"Yes," I said, "and now there can be many Bibles and many truths. Just breathe. Breathe. And please don't panic. This is good! This is wonderful! Just don't panic, and keep breathing in and breathing out. Good. Good. And now can you begin to see how 'the' has been keeping us in a prison in science, in politics, and not just in religion. Because we're always searching for 'the' answer, 'the' origin of man, 'the' cure for cancer, 'the' cause of this and that, and so we've locked ourselves out of ever gaining understanding, and instead are forever just coming up with new, improved shallow theories and arrogant, self-serving opinions.

"Truly, understand that when your heads hit your pillows tonight, you are going to be Goding. No joke. You will once more have Direct Contact with the Almighty, and this is how Our Six Sister Planets finally started moving out of chaos and violence and being lost and began regaining Harmony and Peace with Creation Creating.

"Like I said, words are manmade and limiting within their own definition and they've only been around 40,000 years at best, and so right now words own us. We don't own them. And this has all been part of our ongoing stages of Godelution, so tonight ask your Guardian Angel, your

Genius-Jesusing, for guidance of the Highest Vibrations and you will go on a wonderful adventurous DreamVoyage.

"And also, ask to awake in the morning rested and happy. BIG BIG HAPPY! And Totally at Peace and in Harmony with all the rest of Creation! Ask this, and truly you will RECEIVE, RECEIVE, RECEIVE EVEN FROM THE FURTHEST REACHES OF THE UNIVERSE FOR YOU ARE A HOLLOW BONE! A BUFFALO BONE! AN INSTRUMENT OF GOD-GODING FOR SPREADING HIS/HER LOVE*AMOR* THROUGHOUT ALL THE HEAVENS!"

# BOOK THREE

# Ten

And that night I went right to sleep and I had one of my old flying dream. Once more I was on a dirt road on Mount Palomar just east of our rancho in Oceanside, California. A whole bunch of happy people were with me and we were spreading out our arms into the wind and laughing and laughing like little kids. Then when a great strong gust of wind came up, our arms turned into wings. Magnificent wings! And now we just took a little short run and leaped off the mountain top and we were flying and gliding over the great mountainous land of Southern California, going west to the sea. And at the beach, some of us joined in with the seagulls, but like always, I joined in with the pelicans, and now I, too, was gliding along the crest of the waves. Oh, it felt so free and wonderful and easy! BIG BIG EASY! And thusly, I awoke, feeling WONDERFUL!

I started laughing, I felt so good! Then I smelled wild flowers just as I'd smelled in Madrid, Spain when Jesus had come to me, but this time I didn't see Him. Still I said, "Good morning," and heard Jesus say, "Good Morning," back to me.

Then He said, "We're all very proud of you. You're doing very well."

I laughed. "Thanks, but I'll tell you, I was a little unsure a couple of times yesterday."

"So were we," He said, laughing, too.

"You? But how can You be unsure?"

He laughed all the more.

Then I saw it. "Oh, yeah," I said, "we, Human People, have freewill. I forgot."

And just like that, I couldn't smell the beautiful wild flowers anymore.

I stretched and stretched, and then got up. Oh, I was feeling just fabulous! I went to the bathroom, showered, dressed, and then went out on the balcony to give thanks to the Father Sun, the Right Eye of God, then I went downstairs and I could smell freshly baked rolls and hear laughter before I'd even entered the room where our event was being held. It was Heaven! I could see that as a group, the nuns were bubbling with joy, but a lot of the priests didn't look so good. I guessed that some of them had had a difficult night.

Sister Mary came rushing up and gave me a big hug and kiss each cheek and then so did Sister Margaret and two other nuns, but only Father James and Mark came and greeted me. And big burly Joe just watched Mary and Margaret hug and kiss me, and he shook his head. I waved for him to come over but he just shook his head again. Myself, I wasn't all that hungry this morning and so all I ate was fruit and cottage cheese, and then I went over to the large expand of windows, said "Hello," to the geese and deer, then turned around to everyone.

"Good morning," I said. "Good morning! Good morning! I hope you all slept very well. Myself, I slept like a baby and had a wonderful flying dream, but," I added, "before we start today, I'd like us to form a circle with chairs so we can all be participants. After all, you are all now Geniuses, and so there are no more leaders for we've all accessed our Kingdom of God that Jesus so wisely told us about. And please bring along your coffee and these delicious wonderful rolls that were freshly baked for us this morning. Mmmmmm, good, eh?"

And so everyone brought up their chair, even a couple of priests who seemed pretty reluctant.

"All right," I said, once were all seated, "so how did you all sleep? Like I said, I slept like a baby and had a wonderful flying dream. So I'd now like you all to share, and please give your name when you do. Okay? So who'd like to start?"

Sister Mary instantly raised her hand with a screech of joy!

"So hit it," I said, laughing. "Go for it!"

"Well, my name is Mary, and I'd like to say that usually when I wake up in the middle of the night, I try to go back to sleep, but last night I didn't try to go back to sleep, because I was so excited! So I got up and came down to the kitchen to make myself a cup of coffee and I found Margaret and Eve already there and they, too, were so happy and full of energy, but I only visited with them for a little bit, because I just knew that I had to start writing.

"And they were baking anyway, so I didn't feel bad about leaving them in the kitchen and I went into our den, started a fire in the fireplace, and I could barely contain myself, because all these great ideas and insights just kept coming to me. I felt Blessed! I felt like I'd finally really Awakened! And I bet that this is how you felt when you were writing *Rain of Gold*," she added.

I laughed. "Yes, exactly, everyday was Christmas with all these great insights that were being gifted to me every morning from Heaven."

"Yes, this is exactly how I felt this morning," said Mary. "And I hadn't felt like that since I was a very young nun!"

I took in a great big deep breath. "That's wonderful, Mary," I said, "and I'd like you to Know that writing, that keeping a journal, is, in fact, Bibling, and that Bibling is our salvation. Bill, not Shakespeare, but Bill Cartwright my longest best friend who hiked into the Rain of Gold canyon with me that first time and has been a family counselor for over 30 years, he has always told me that the opposite of depression is expression, and when you write down what you're feeling deep inside, you then instantly make room for new possibilities to come into your life. And this is what you were doing, Mary. You giving Birth to God! Because like I said earlier my *mamagrande* always explained to me that we come into this world, into this dimension of reality, pregnant with the Holy Creator, and so this is our Holy Job."

"Then you equate writing a journal to writing the Bible?" asked a priest.

"Sure. What is the Bible? It's a group of stories that connect a tribe to God and Creation, and this is what Mary did last night, and Anne Frank did, and we all do when we get up in the middle of the night and the Stars, our *Familia*, are talking to us. Like Mary said, she felt Blessed. She felt like she'd finally Awakened. And hopefully you'll feel the same thing soon. You see, it took me four months of not talking to get to where Mary got in just one night." I turned back to Mary. "Thank you," I said. "You're on your way, Mary. You are doing your Holy Work here on

Mother Earth, which is, of course, to give Birth to God, to give Life to God with All your Life within your very own Kingdom of God that Jesus was sent here to tell us about."

"Yes!" she said. "This is exactly what I was feeling! It's like I Awoke with this great excitement to give Voice, to give Life to all the Goodness that I could feel that I was Receiving in Abundance from the whole Universe! A Hollow Bone I'd become! A Buffalo Bone I'd become! And yet I could never have allowed myself to feel any of this until I understood that Everything is a Verb and that Creation is still going on. It was like my life had reopened in a way I haven't felt since I was a young nun and the bride of my Lord Jesus Christ! Oh, I Awoke with such feeling of ecstasy and warmth and joy and all these feelings and thoughts that, I guess, I'd been holding back for all these years, they now came flooding back to me! Oh, I can hardly wait to go back to sleep tonight, so I can Awake again and continue feeling like I'm once more Directly Receiving from God through his Son Jesus!"

"WONDERFUL!" I said. "WONDERFUL! And so how many of you also Awoke in the middle of the night feeling like this?"

Three more nuns raised their hands, but not one priest.

"I never even got to sleep," said the priest who'd asked if I equated journaling to Bibling. "And what kept me up was, well, why YOU?" He was angry.

"Why me?" I said, taking in a deep breath.

"Yes, why you!" he repeated. "I don't see you as being that special, or educated, or anything else!"

"Why me, eh?" I said, closing my eyes so I wouldn't have to keep looking at this priest's angry face, and I could keep focused. "Well, I'd like you to know that I used to ask myself this same question? I mean, I'd meet people who were slender and all smiles and very spiritual looking and didn't swear, didn't drink *tequila,* didn't look at women and were vegetarian, and they didn't lose their temper, and I say why not them? They're certainly much nicer people than me. But then I remembered that I wasn't a very good wrestler, either, and yet as a freshman I tied the senior who took the California State Championship. And in chess, I beat all the smartest students at school, plus all the faculty, and then it came to me that the real question is not why not them, but why NOT me. Because by asking why not them, I was giving away all of my Powers to them over there and leaving me here, inside, with *nada, nada,* nothing. And by asking why not me with All of my Heart and Soul, I was then in a flash bringing in All of the Powers of the Universe into me! And this is what Johann Wolfgang von Goethe wrote about when he so brilliantly said: 'Whatever you can do or dream you can do, begin it! Boldness has genius, power, and magic!"

"Well, yes," he said, "but—"

I raised up my open hand, palm towards him, closing my eyes, and said in a loud voice, "Please, no 'but' here! Let me finish what I'm saying, because you have asked a very important question! Either we start empowering ourselves, or . . . or we just keep finger pointing at others, passing judgment, and never take in our full potential, because by you asking this question tells me that you, sir, have over and over chickened out on your OWN POWERS!"

I stopped, opened my eyes, staring at him eye to eye and took in a deep breath. "For instance," I said, "take my last confession back in 1959 when I was 19 years. It's well documented in my book *CrazyLoco Love.*"

"You haven't been to confession for 40 years?" he barked at me.

"No, I haven't, and that's not the point!" I barked back. "The point is I started taking my powers back then, and I didn't realize it until later. You see, I did my last confession at the Chapel of the Catholic University of San Diego where I was going to school, and . . . and it suddenly came to me that yes, I could confess my sins for the Love of God, but not for Fear of God and the pains of hell. And so I said no to that priest, telling him that I would not say that, that I'd rather burn in hell for all eternity than to think for one moment that I was suppose to fear God and believe that . . . that the Almighty would ever even create such a place as hell.

"I was pumped! I was ready to burn for All Eternity, but I would not back down, and finally the priest was so exasperated at me that he said that if I didn't say that, then I couldn't be a Catholic. This had never entered my mind, but when he said this to me, I then said, "GOOD! GREAT! Then I'm no longer a Catholic!" And I opened up the little curtains of the confessional and stepped out. He got out, too, and started telling me that I just couldn't do that, because I'd been baptized and I'd gone to confirmation and etc. and etc. And I said to him, "Hey, Father, I don't have to listen to anything you tell me anymore, because I'm no longer a Catholic. Goodbye!"

"And I turned and went running and shouting with joy out of the Chapel, and outside I'd never seen the world so beautiful! And that's the night I looked up the word catholic in my Webster Dictionary to find out what I wasn't anymore, and to my shock, I found that it didn't just say universal as we Catholics were always being told, but it also said, 'all-inclusive, of general interest and values and having broad sympathies and understanding; hence, liberal.'

"I screamed with joy, because then I was a real catholic! I REALLY REALLY WAS! And this old priest who'd insisted that I had to have fear of God wasn't a real catholic, because being a catholic meant not just universal, but all-inclusive and having broad understandings and sympathies and so this included me, and so I got in my car and drove over to my cousin's apartment in Ocean Beach where he lived with a bunch of ex-G.I.s, who were also students at the Catholic University, and I told them what had happened and showed them the definition of catholic in my Webster, and instead of rejoicing, they asked me to leave when I wouldn't stop talking so excitedly.

"And those big strong ex-soldiers, who were all older than me, reported me to the priests and the priests informed my parents, but I would not back down, because like I kept telling them, once you get past the Fear of God, then you automatically only see the Absolute Joy and Unconditional Love of God and All, All, All of Creation! The Stars Sing! The Ocean Waves Dance! And the Flowers and Trees smell of Heaven, and for the first time in all my life, I felt Whole and Connected and Happy and FREE!

"So why me? Well, I'll tell you, because I didn't ask why about anyone else and because there are no accidents. Particularly in the Spirit World, and this incident, I'm sure, was what helped prepare me for what Harry Walters and Jack Big Shoulders told me in Nashville, because I was able to grasp what it was that they meant when they told me that they didn't believe in God, that they did God, and they lived with God like my *mamagrande* had lived with *Papito Dios!*

"You see, to go even further, 'belief' is a weak word. You don't 'believe' in your car. You Know you car. And to Know is strong. To 'believe' is weak. It takes us out of the realm of concrete solid knowledge and responsibility, and gives us something to hide behind, because you can't argue with belief, and a person can believe anything they want, and cover up their real agenda. And on the other hand, by doing God by first Walking in Beauty, and then by Harmonizing with All of Creation, then actually Being God-Goding when you find Peace with a capital 'P' within yourself, Totally, Totally makes you Responsible for Everything you Do and you Think. Right Here! Right Now! The buck stops with you!

"Do you see—no, I mean feel what I'm saying? You no longer pass judgment on others. You no longer use the Bible so you can be righteous and full of contempt for others. Eh, are you with me? Like you no longer see handicapped children as even being handicapped. You now see them as Holy Gifts straight from God-Goding that are giving you the opportunity to see the Light of Goding in Everything and Everyone, Equally!" Tears came to my eyes. "You no longer see Down syndrome kids as weird-looking, but as so God-Goding Beautiful with their Big Smiles and Innocent Joy, because you now start doing as the Native Tribes of Central America say when they meet someone, particularly a stranger, 'You are another me, and I am another you,' and you then put your hands behind your back and touch foreheads.

"And homeless people in them I see me and my dad and his poor old Indian mother coming to the Texas border, starving and desperate, and I also remember that my dad went to prison at 13 for stealing six dollars worth of copper ore from the Copper Queen Mining Company of Douglas, Arizona, so he could feed his starving family." Tears were pouring down my face. "So why me, because I asked that question about me, myself, and not you or anyone else and this is what opened up the Flood Gates to All the Powers of the Universe so they could come pouring into me. And I was then able to make a deal with the Almighty to become a writer as great as Homer and/or greater and I didn't even know how to read!

"And why? Because since then I've learned again and again that when we finally see All, All, All People in Ourselves, and especially in the most looked down upon by our society, we then become a VEHICLE OF THE GREATEST ENERGY FORCE AVAILABLE TO US HUMAN BEINGS! Truly, this is why *Of Mice and Men* by John Steinbeck is such a great book! It opens our HeartEyes! And why *The Diary of Anne Frank* is so moving, and *Los de Abajo* by Azuela. So why me? YOU TELL ME! You open up your HeartEyes and see me as you. And special! And wonderful! And as a gift straight from God-Goding! Because this is how I SEE YOU, AND WE ALL, ALL, ALL NEED TO START SEEING EACH OTHER AS, INDEED, ANOTHER US!"

I quit.

I couldn't stop crying, this answer had totally drained me. He looked stunned. He just kept staring at me.

"Look," he finally said. "I'm sorry. I really am. I just thought that you were all about wanting to be an author and famous."

I burst out laughing and laughing. "Oh, my God," I said. "Tell me, have you even read *Rain of Gold*?"

He suddenly looked like a little mouse that'd just been caught in a trap. "I think I better, well, just shut up," he said, glancing around and seeing how everyone was staring at him. "I'm sorry."

"No, please don't be sorry," I said, still laughing and wiping the tears out of my eyes. "It was a question that probably needed to be asked. I'm sure others have been thinking the same thing, but didn't have, well, the guts to ask. Okay, who else?"

Another priest raised his hand.

"Go on," I said.

"Matt," he said, "and I, too, didn't sleep the whole night, but what kept coming to me was that you said you didn't sleep for two years. So I finally got dressed and went for a walk, and, well, quite honestly, I began to wonder if you'd been on drugs when you had all of these experiences, because, well," he said, turning red, "I dropped acid when I was a teenager and we went to visit relatives out in Santa Monica, California. And what I experienced, frightened me so much that I never took any drugs again, and especially not after one of my cousins in California died from an overdose. So my question to you is this, do you do drugs?"

"Okay," I said, "I'll answer you, but I first need to put this in perspective. As a rule I drink. I don't do drugs, and yet I've taken *peyote* a couple of times in Native American ceremonies with compete supervision and ritual. And I've done mushrooms once in the same way, and I smoke grass now and then with friends."

"How often?"

"Oh, maybe four or five times a year, because what I do on a regular basis is drink. But now," I said, "getting to your real question, was I under the influence when I've had any of my Miraculous Experiences? No, not even a little bit. I was totally clean and sober."

"Okay," he said, "before last night I wouldn't have believed you, but since what happened to me last night, I'm now inclined to believe you, because I swear that the trees began singing to me just as they had when I'd dropped that acid, and then the stars began waltzing, and . . . and everything was alive! Totally alive with light and color and so beautiful! And yet I didn't have the fear that I'd had as a teenager. In fact, I felt at peace, and then I began to hear music, a symphony, and I remembered that you said that when God created the Universe He created one verse, one song, and that we all came into manifestation with our own Song, and so I understood that for the first time in my life, that I do have my own Song, and this is what I was hearing and it was making me so happy! Like you say, BIG BIG HAPPY!"

Tears of joy were running down his face, and I went across the room and took Matt in my arms, hugging and kissing him, then I stepped away.

"You, my dear *amigo*," I said, "have just become a Sacred Elder!"

"Me? A Sacred Elder?"

"Yes, you and Mary have Awakened, and become Sacred Elders! Because to be a Sacred Elder is to be in Tune with your own Holy Song that you brought with you from the Heavens along with your Guardian Angel. And so now as Sacred Elders you and Mary need to come out of retirement, and SHOOT INTO INSPIREMENT! For you are now in Harmony with the HOLY MUSIC OF GOD-GODING!"

"You know, maybe you're right," said Matt. "I do feel like this is now a whole new beginning for me."

"It is," I said, with tears of joy streaming down my face, too. "I remember what my good friend Louis L'Amour, the western writer, once said to me. 'There will come a time when you believe everything is finished, and that will be the beginning.' And Mr. L'Amour, who finally even outsold John Steinbeck, KNEW what he was talking about. You, my *amigo*-friend and Mary, *mi amiga*, have AWOKEN! Shooting past all Fear and you are now Ghosting, SongShifting, and Miracle Making just as *Espirito* who followed a deer and her fawn in search of water in the first sentence of *Rain of Gold*. And when *Espirito*, meaning Little Spirit, saw the sunlight reflecting off the waterfall in the early morning light, he said, 'It's a rain of gold!' and thusly it became, and that first sentence used to be 300 words long, but I finally had to just simplify it or I would have lost all my readers, and especially the ones who only spoke English.

"Congratulations! For you two are now Living with one foot on This Side and another foot on the Other Side, and you two are now Living, Breathing *Espiritos* just like that old Indian in *Rain of Gold*! Can you feel it? Is all this finally beginning to make sense to you two? For you two are now Co-Creators with God-Goding, and ready to travel to the Red City of the Americas where All Sacred Elders and Holy *Curanderos* used to travel to before Columbus. And this Red City, some believe was at the great pyramids outside of Mexico City and other scholars are now beginning to think it was the pyramids that are now just being excavated by Guatemala.

"Anyway, Sacred Elders and Holy Healers would come from South America and North America to this Red City and for 10 years they'd exchange Sacred Knowledge and Interplanetary Wisdom with parrots listening, and then they'd go back north and south for 10 years spreading this Sacred Knowledge of Being Interplanetary Miracle Makers. Like Creating a Rainstorm when a drought came, like healing people by chanting and bringing their Holy Song back into Harmony with the Sympathy of God-Goding. Because you see, disease originally meant not-at-ease, and so when a Human is Totally-at-Ease, Totally-in-Tune with their God-Given-Song, then BINGO! All diseases disappear! And so this is now your calling, your Holy Work as Sacred Elders and Holy Healers to help Human People and Our Mother Earth Heal Themselves Spiritually and Physically."

Tears of joy were pouring down Matt's face.

"You're right," he said. "You're absolutely right! I was there at that Red City last night and I heard the Symphony of Creation, but still, I'm sure I'll probably go, well, not two years without sleeping like you did, but at least a week—I'M SO EXCITED!"

"Myself," said Mary, "I didn't go to the Red City, but I'm so happy and excited that I'm going to go the rest of my life without sleeping! Oh, this is WONDERFUL! And I can now see that your Great Great Great Great Great Aunt, Mother Of No Specific Child could have easily lived to the age of 165. How could she not when she was Goding!"

All the nuns were up on their feet and cheering, and then congratulating Matt and Mary with hugs and kisses. And big burly Joe was just watching. So I finally walked over and got hold of him, and came pulling him across the room and threw him into the mass of hugging, kissing people.

And there was *Margarita* in the middle of the whole thing, and when she turned and saw big Joe, she opened up her arms to him, but he was so shocked that at first he didn't know what to do. But then this face burst into a huge smile, and he went for it, hugging this woman that he'd been in love with for over 60 years!

# Eleven

We took a break. I went to my room, put on my running shoes, and then took off running around the lake. I'd been running for nearly 40 years, ever since I'd taken up wrestling in high school and I usually ran about 20 to 25 miles a week. Four runs of about three to four miles, then one day a week I'd go a 10 mile distance, and on these runs, I'd do the first mile at about an eight minute pace, then I'd drop down to a seven minute pace, and at this faster speed I'd no longer be jogging but running, and it would be easier on my knees because I'd be using the front part of my feet more, and pushing off with my toes and so it felt like sailing!

Oh, I loved running! It was a natural high! And also, right now, I'd get to be alone, so I could let things kind of catch up with me, because oh, boy, had we just covered a lot of ground. Never in a million years did I ever dream that these old farts—I mean these old nuns and priest would be so Alive and Open and Available!

But then up ahead, who did I see, it was Mark and he was running, too, and really kicking ass. And normally I would've pushed myself dropping to an under 6 minute pace to catch the person and/or people ahead of me, but I didn't. I stayed well behind and just followed Mark as he went on trails through the woods and alongside creeks and it was wonderful. Once we jumped a herd of deer, and we came back laughing, but never having said a word until we'd returned. I was the first to speak.

"So how did it go for you last night, Mark?" I asked.

He took in a deep breath. "Very productive," he said, "and yet very strange, but I'd like to save my comments for the group," he added.

"Okay," I said, and we parted and I went up to my room, took a quick shower, and then went back downstairs.

Instantly, I could feel the difference. The whole room felt in Harmony and Alive and Full of Love Amor! Even the priests as a group, now seemed happy and relaxed. People were talking excitedly and laughing and having a very good time!

I got myself a cup of hot water and brought out my lavender Yogi Licorice tea bag. I sat down in our circle of chairs and began dunking my tea bag up and down in the hot water until it was a golden color. I never drank coffee or caffeinated tea. I was always already so naturally high that if I felt any better I'd probably get arrested. Seeing me sit down, the others began taking their seats, too.

"Okay," I said, once everyone was seated, "as you can all see we've become a pretty relaxed happy group."

A priest raised his hand.

"Okay," I said. "Go on."

"Have you ever read the book *The Outsider* by Colin Wilson?" he asked.

I shook my head.

"I think you should," he said. "Because what Wilson does, is that he gives us understanding of the human mind and shows us how the human mind can only handle so much before it, well, cracks, or goes insane. And he uses the examples of Van Gogh, Vaslav Nijinsky, Lawrence,

Rimbaud, T.S. Eliot, all these gifted heavyweights of the arts, and so not only did I have trouble sleeping last night, but I ended up throwing up my whole dinner." Tears were streaming down his face "And what kept coming to me, from deep inside of me, was, well, if we do, in fact, take 'the' away from the Bible, then does this mean that you're suggesting that we take 'the' away from what Jesus Christ told us about Him being 'the' only way?"

I took in a deep breath and closed my eyes, asking for guidance. This was a big one. Maybe even the biggest one, because this one hit the nail right on the head of our entire Western Civilization. I took in more deep breaths and suddenly I smelled wild flowers, and so I once more Knew that Our Lord Jesus was here with us. I opened my eyes, and no, I couldn't see Jesus, but I could sure feel His Full Powers of Love*Amor* nothing but Love*Amor* and His Sacred Energy was going up and down my spine with a Tingling Sensations that got so hot that I began sweating.

"Well," I said, turning to this priest. "I can well understand why this would be a pretty disturbing thought, because I, too, got pretty upset when this notion first came to me. But then I prayed and asked for guidance, turning it all over to God."

"BUT!" he yelled. "How can I now turn it all over to God through His Only Son Jesus, if we take 'the' away?"

I closed my eyes and took in a deep breath, smelling the Wild Flowers, and then another deep breath, smelling these most wonderful smelling Wild Flowers again, and I now opened my eyes, feeling Totally Connected.

"Excuse me," I said, "but with whom am I speaking?"

"Oh, Adam," he said. "Sorry. I forgot. I haven't been thinking very clearly."

"Well, Adam," I said, getting out of my chair and moving back by the large expanse of windows, so I wouldn't be affected by his energy, "you know, I'm being told right now . . . that what you need to do is to find this answer on your own. Because, for me, to tell you my answer wouldn't be a good fit, and this is a big one. Maybe even 'the' biggest for most Christians."

"All right, but how do I do this?" he asked once again. "Last night, I swear, I felt so confused and upset that it was even difficult for me to pray. I kept losing focus, because so much of what you've shared with us seems true, and even feels true, and also, I read your whole book more than once, and so . . . well, I just don't know what to do, because I'm afraid that if I lose my Church and the whole structure that I've been brought up with, I might lose God and end up cutting off not just one ear, BUT BOTH EARS!"

He stopped and took in several deep breaths, and blew out fast each time. "I now realize why there was a very large part of me that was against having you come to see us. We're old! We're retired! And so we just want to make peace within us, so we can—"

He was trembling, and tears were pouring down his face, but he wasn't bothering to wipe them off. I walked over to him and took the white handkerchief out of my back pocket that I always carried that my mother had given me years ago and had little red flowers and green leaves that she'd embroidered on it.

"Here," I said, "from my mother to you."

"Thank you," he said, taking the white handkerchief and wiping his eyes.

"No, thank you," I said. "For Totally Opening your Whole Heart and Soul."

He laughed. "Trust me, I didn't mean to," he said. "It just all came out."

"Yes, and that's the way it normally is in giving and in receiving. For this is who we, Human Beings, really are, Holy Instruments of God."

"There!" he shouted. "YOU'VE DONE IT AGAIN! And this is awful, because I really did love *Rain of Gold* and I really do love all that you've told us, but it also, well, destroys the Church! MY CHURCH! THE WHOLE WORLD'S CHURCH! Just look what all this profound thinking has done to you! You're not even Catholic anymore!"

The whole room was silent. Adam had certainly brought everything back to square one. Then *Margarita* spoke with such a gentle tone that it helped us all to regain composure.

"Does it really destroy the Church?" she asked. "Or does it help Our Beloved Church to become what it originally professed to be, universal and all-inclusive."

"BUT THAT'S NOT WHAT JESUS OR THE BIBLE SAY!" shouted Adam.

"Excuse me," I said, "but you do know that most scholars now agree that Jesus spoke Aramaic when he was with us here on earth."

"Yes, I understand that," said Adam.

"Well," I said, "there is no word 'the' in the Aramaic Language."

"What? What are you saying?"

"I'm saying," I said, "that Jesus never said that He was 'the' only way. The Greek's translation added 'the' and 'only' was added by the English. So Our Lord Jesus said that He was 'a way', and/or He simply said He was 'way', and so His message was Totally about Inclusion and He was inviting All of Us to Be Sons and Daughters of God,

Equally. Even the Romans and not just the Jews. And this only makes sense, because the Roman Empire controlled the whole known world and Jesus, Son of God, wanted to bring Peace to the Whole World just as He wants to do today."

Adam bent over, gripping his stomach. "Then you're really serious about all this you've shared with us, even about the Vatican mo – mo!" He began gagging, but nothing was coming up.

Mark and *Margarita* rushed to help Adam over to a couch to lie down, and his body continued trembling and jerking.

"Okay," I said, "is anyone else feeling kind of sick."

Half a dozen hands went up.

"You know," said another priest, "if we'd been told all this as young seminarians I'm quite sure we wouldn't have had any trouble accepting all this, because it does make sense. Why would the Son of God not invite us all to become sons and daughters of the Holy Creator equally? And I can also see how this could revolutionize the whole Church and help unite all the different religions of the world. So yes, I can see all this in my mind. I really can. But here, in my gut, I'm too old to accept any of this. I agree with Adam. You've come to us 50 to 60 years too late and what we now want is peace and tranquility."

"And you are who?" I asked.

"Oh, excuse me, Michael," he said.

"And how old are you Michael?" I asked.

"I'm 80," he said.

"Look," I said, "you're only 80. You've only been into the most perfect age of 78 for two little years, so come on, stop bullshitting yourself and realize that you're just getting started and you have a RESPONSIBILITY OF BECOMING A SACRED ELDER!" I shouted, startling the shit out of him.

"But look what just happened to Adam," he said sheepishly, "and to Van Gogh. There's only so much that the human mind can take."

"You're right," I said. "There is only so much that the human mind can take. But you now Know that we don't just process information with our mind and 4 senses. You now Know that we have 3 centers for processing information, and with our Full Natural 13 Senses, then there are no limitations. Van Gogh, Nijinsky, Rimbaud, all of these guys would have had no *problemas* if their Full Natural 13 Senses had been firing."

"Really, you think so?"

"I KNOW SO!" I yelled. "And you Know it was a capital 'K', too! Look, Western Civilization is like a big 12 cylinder engine that's only using 4 of its cylinders, so, of course, it's easy to go berserk. And also note, all those who broke down were men, not women, and Anne Frank and my two *mamagrandes* endured 10,000 times more horror and confusion and still they didn't go insane, but instead THESE WOMEN ROSE UP WITH THEIR FULL POWERS AS ANGELS STRAIGHT FROM GOD!

"So no! You will not check out! You are 80 years and Totally, Totally Available! So stand up! Come on, get your ass out of that chair, and LEAP into your Balanced Female and Male Energies and take on your RESPONSIBILITY of becoming a Sacred ELDER! There's no turning back for you guys! You took an oath to Be Of Service for God-Goding, and so you now keep your word, because you see, the aging process from a Spiritual Point of View starts reversing when you reach the age of 65 and you have Balanced your Male and Female Energies! And so you are 65 going on 55, and then 75 going on 60, then 80 going on 65, then 104 going on 78, because Spirit Aging can actually override physical aging to the degree that you accept your Full God-Given Spirituality. Tell him, Mary! Tell him, Matt! Tell Michael about all this Fantastic Great Youthful Energy that came BURSTING into you two last night!"

And so Mary told him that she was 86 and she, too, had thought she was over the hill, that her days of service were over, but then last night all these great feelings of Love*Amor* had come BURSTING into her Heart and Soul, and she now felt as Full of Energy and Purposeful as when she'd been a young nun.

"And I can now see," she said to Michael, "that I'd lost faith, well, not in God, but in my ability to make any difference, because of all the undermining politic of clerical life and all the terrible news that we see on T.V."

"Exactly," said Matt, "but now with the Vatican moving to Ireland for 100 years, and then to Mexico where my grandparents were from for another 100 years, has sent my whole world into such a spin of WONDERFUL POSSIBILITIES, that if I just keep calm and don't let myself go into fear or doubt, then I'm flying in ECSTASY WITH SUCH ENERGY that I, too, now feel like a young bride of Our Lord Jesus! And also remember, the Vatican was moved to France for nearly a century," he added. "So there has been a precedent."

"No, that's not true," said Michael. "What happened was that the King of France appointed his own Pope. And what Mr. Villaseñor is suggesting is that the Vatican itself be moved to Ireland. Is this correct?" he said, turning to me.

I nodded. "Yes, this was part of the information that was Transmitted into me in Madrid."

"When Jesus came to you?" said Michael with a tone of sarcasm.

"Yes," I said, refusing to be taken in by his energy.

"And it makes SO MUCH SENSE!" shouted Matt excitedly. "Because back then our whole known world was centered around the Mediterranean Sea, and so Italy, Rome, seemed the logical location to place the head of the Catholic Church, but now with what we know of the entire globe, it only makes sense to move the Vatican, and then keep moving the location of the head of the Catholic Church every 100 years around the globe! OH, THIS IS SO EXCITING! I SEE IT! I ACTUALLY SEE IT ALREADY DONE!"

"YES!" I said. "AND WRITTEN IN THE STARS! The Future doesn't necessarily come after the Present. Time is circular. And this moment is already a long forgotten memory in the furthest reaches of the UNIVERSE!"

"HE'S RIGHT!" shouted Matt. "And Our Lord Jesus is with us RIGHT HERE! RIGHT NOW! He's never left us! Oh, I can SEE IT ALL SO CLEARLY! This is WONDERFUL! And Gaelic makes perfect sense! And then in Mexico an Indian dialect of the Yucatan. Yes, the language of your Great Great Great Aunt Mother Of No Specific Child! And in doing all this, Our Holy Catholic Church becomes of Goding. Not of men. But of men and of women with us having Women Popes and Women Cardinals and Women Bishops, and . . . and can't you all see it? Our Church becomes Sacred and Forever Changing and . . . and will then continue for 52,000 years? Could this be right?" he asked.

"It's perfectly right," I said, "because Our Mother Earth works in 26,000 year cycles. One cycle being of male energy like we're just completing, and the other being of female energy that we are just starting. And so 52,000 years is one complete cycle of male and female energy, and by lasting for 52,000 years, Our Holy Church will then be in the Sacred Flow of Creation Creating, and hence, Eternal! And this is exactly what Jesus was Transmitting into me in Madrid, Spain back in November of 1992 when *mi familia* and I and a group of Native American went to Spain to forgive the queen and king for all of the atrocities that Spain committed around the globe, and then plant a Snow Goose Global Thanksgiving Flag from World-Wide Harmony and Peace and Abundance for All!

"And Jesus came to me in my little hotel room where I'd lain down to take a nap, because I'd lost my focus. My thinking head had taken over and so I was full of thinking and doubt, and then when I awoke, I could see that there was a man at the far end of my little room and he was surrounded by a bright golden light that lit up the whole room and yet was soft and didn't hurt my eyes.

"All this is being well documented in the book *Beyond Rain of Gold* I'm presently re-writing, and suddenly I Knew with a capital 'K' that this was Jesus, and so I got up on my elbows to see Him better and I could see that He was hovering about two feet off the floor. And I got up and this was when He reached into His chest and brought out His Most Holy Sacred Heart. A real pulsating heart with arteries and everything and He reached out handing me His Heart, and in the act of doing this, He changed into all the different Human People of the world. In features. In skin color. In robes. In eyes. In everything. And this was when I Knew that Jesus is in Everyone of Us. You, Me, We, ALL OF US! And I was no longer lost and I KNEW EXACTLY, EXACTLY why we'd come to Spain and what we were to do, and WE DID IT! WE REALLY DID!"

"What did you do?"

"Oh, my God!" I said. "I need to lie down, and/or have a beer and a *tequila*. Wow! Let's just call it a day, and we'll get into all this *mañana*. Because, remember, tomorrow is *otro milagro de Dios*!"

Mark raised his hand. "Excuse me," he said, looking at me, "but when we got back from running you asked me how it went for me last night. And I told you very productive, and yet very strange, and that I didn't want to say anything to you about it, because I wanted to share it for our group."

I nodded. "Okay, so please do share."

He stood up. "You see," he said, turning to everyone, "I'm not here because I had a nervous breakdown as some of you might believe. I'm here, because, well, I, too, proposed to a nun and she accepted, and so we are now both leaving the Church so we can marry. And I'll tell you," he said, taking in a deep breath, " I'm so much in love with *Josefina*, whom I met in Ecuador, that my whole world has changed, and I've come to the realization that Our Holy Lord God-Goding can be nothing but Love*Amor*, and that all there is is LOVE*Amor* THROUGHOUT THE UNIVERSE!

"You see, I'd never heard of Mr. Villaseñor or of his writings. Then I came here and our Sisters were talking about nothing else, and so I read *Rain of Gold* not once, but well over five times so far, and I now see that what I saw in our Native American Sisters of Ecuador is what

*Rain of Gold* is really all about. Just like his two beloved grandmothers, *Doña Guadalupe* and *Doña Margarita,* were so full of Wisdom and Pure *Amor* and an Indestructible Faith in the Almighty, so are our Sisters in Ecuador.

"And it troubled me, because our American and European Sisters are good-hearted wonderful people, too, and yet I could feel that something was missing, but I had no idea what that something was until now that Mr. Villaseñor, himself, told us that even he, who wrote *Rain of Gold*, didn't understand his own book until that Navajo and that Lakota Indians explained his own book to him. Then I understood. Language, languaging truly does own us, as Mr. Villaseñor stated.

"And also it makes sense that we have more than 5 senses. For instance, when I was about 10 years old, my younger brother Luke suddenly awoke in the middle of the night and started telling us that our dad had had a car accident and that he was dying, and so we had to pray, so he wouldn't die! My mother and I and my sisters and little brother all started praying, and we received a call about an hour later that our dad had been in a terrible wreck, and yet miraculously he was going to be okay.

"And so, what I'm saying with all this . . . is that with our Natural Multi-Sensory Perception of our Full 13 Senses and our understanding that Creation is still going on at this very moment, then that experience my younger brother had becomes available to all of us. And this is Our Future, Our Destiny, for the Perception of the Miraculous to become part of Our Norm.

"Look, now that I Know that we have 3 Centers for processing information and experience, I'm feeling Complete. I'm feeling Whole. Because I can now see that

the Thinking Brain Center truly is our smallest computer. And now with Our Intuitive Heart Center and Our
Psychic Soul Center, I really do feel LIMITLESS! And
closer to God! And so we need to start including all this
in the teachings at our Catholic Schools, so that our kids
can then start Genius-Jesusing!"

He stopped and tears of joy, of ecstasy were pour-
ing down this face. "What a concept Jesus-Geniusing!
What Possibilities! What Energy! What Purity! What—oh,
my God-Goding! This is all so wonderful! It's like ALL,
ALL, ALL OF ME HAS BECOME ALIVE AND I'M NOW
COMPLETE! Because . . . because I'm no longer 'with'
Jesus. I am now 'of' Jesus, and so I, too, am now Son of
God-Goding! And I can now see that this was the something that was missing with my American and European
Sisters and Priests. We 'believed' in Miracles, but we didn't
'Know' Miracles, and so we could never then 'Do' Miracles,
because we were 'with' Jesus and not 'of' Jesus, and we
were also perceiving reality within our limited scope of 5
senses. But then with Being Of Jesus and perceiving life
with Our Full Natural 13 Senses and the understanding
that Creations is still happening, then not only will we
be educating our youth to 'Know' Miracles, but to start
'DOING' MIRACLES! And Jesus told us that what He
did, we would do more, and we can!

"Oh, I can now see so clearly that it has been the
limitations of our European-based languages that have
been holding us back, and once we switch to Gaelic that
something missing in all of us Priests and Nuns will
disappear."

"Exactly!" I said, "and what happened to Adam just
now will stop happening, because Adam was trying to

process everything with just his Head Center, instead of going to his Heart and Soul Centers, too."

"Yes," said Mark, "and so I can also see that the time has come for All of Us Catholics to come out of hiding behind archaic dogma, and take on the whole definition of what it means to Be a Real Catholic with the whole definition of all-inclusive and of general interest and value, having broad sympathies and understanding, hence liberal, and this will move Us into the Light of God-Goding by accepting what Albert Einstein proved, that all there is, is change, and Creation never stopped and never began, and is ongoing Right Here. Right Now. Forever Within Creation Creating. And this isn't just our only hope, but OUR RESPONSIBILITY AS CATHOLICS, AND TRUE FOLLOWERS OF JESUS CHRIST!"

He stopped and took in a deep breath. "Then with feeling all this," he said, "I got up to go to the bathroom and all these flashes of insight kept coming to . . . me and I glanced in the mirror and I saw that we don't just come into this world with a Guardian Angel, as Mr. Villaseñor's grandmother told him, but I saw in the mirror THAT I AM AN ANGEL! THAT WE ALL ARE!"

"I had the same experience!" shouted Mary. "But I was too embarrassed to say it! Mark is ABSOLUTELY right! We're all Angels! It's just we don't Know it until we Awaken!

"I totally agree!" said Matt.

"Me, too," said Joe. "And now I also agree that all there is, is Love*Amor* and nothing but Love*Amor, a*nd it's our own fears and doubts that have been creating evil for us all of these centuries. After all, 'evil' is just 'live' spelled backwards and the 'devil' is just 'lived' spelled backwards. And so it only makes sense that we've been living ass backwards, and so this is what we have been seeing in the mirror! We carry evil and we see evil. We carry the Light of an Angel and we see—"

"We see the Light of an Angel," said several nuns along with big Joe.

And one of these nuns was *Margarita,* and she came across the room to Joe with so much Love*Amor* that her whole person was ILLUMINATING LIGHT! And this time, Joe wasn't shocked, and he took her in his arms and they were hugging and kissing, but not just on the cheeks.

Time stood still.

And we all just watched and tears of joy came to our eyes. She was 91. He was 86. And they'd known each other for over 60 years and now at last they were holding each other and kissing like teenagers. Then they became self conscious and slightly embarrassed and just stood together holding hands, and started giggling.

"And," said Mark, "I almost wasn't going to share all this, but look at the results it has gotten. So are you two," he continued, "going to join *Josefina* and me and also get married. I think you should. Remember, this is a very emotionally-driven planet and so this "Well, if it's a must," said Joe, "then I guess we MUST!"

"Yes, we do want to do our share of helping to Heal Our Mother Earth, and since she is very emotionally-driven, then, well, Joe and I will have to . . . KISS ABOUT IT! " she added, giggling.

"Just look at us," said Mark. "Turn around and just look at each other. We're all Angels! We really are! And this is why Mr. Villaseñor came to us. To show us that Our Holy Catholic Church didn't lose Her way because of ill-intent, but simply because of the empire-based non-emotional language that She's been using for all these centuries for expressing Herself. And so, of course, it only makes sense that the way for Our Beloved Holy Church to come back to Being of Heart and Soul is for Her to move locations and keep moving locations and learning a new Native Languaging every 100 years!

"And so I can now see that it was no accident that I was sent to Ecuador and I fell in Love, and it's no accident I was sent here for the 6 months in which *Josefina* and I can have no contact with each other. And it's no accident that I was introduced to *Rain of Gold*, and it's no accident that you brilliant good Sisters had Mr. Villaseñor come to us. For everything that he has shared with us; we, all of us, already Knew deep inside our own Kingdom of God, which we just hadn't activated, and couldn't activate until we understood that Creation is still happening and that we are 'of' Jesus and not just 'with' Jesus.

"Truly, to move our Holy Church to Ireland and to start 'Being Of Jesus' makes Total Sense. And not because I'm Irish, but because, remember, Ireland saved Western Civilization by keeping all the records and books through the Dark Ages, and then what did the English do? Starve us. Enslave us though indentured servitude. Yes, Ireland, then Mexico, who's suffered even more, then the Philippines, of course, and the Purity of Love*Amor* for God-Goding, a Verb, will be re-established, and these last 2,000 years will then be nothing compared to our Grand Fabulous All-Inclusive Future of Our Great Church! And then *Josefina* and I can be married and we don't have to leave the Church, and Joe, you and *Margarita* can do the same.

"OH, I AWOKE LAUGHING, I felt so happy with all that Mr. Villaseñor has been sharing with us!" Mark shouted. "And then I looked in the mirror and saw that I've become my very own Guardian Angel, and I Knew that yes, I'd come across the Universe gathering Stardust to help God-Goding plant His Ongoing Garden of Heaven on Earth. And so I say Thank You, Thank You, God-Goding for orchestrating this Whole Living, Breathing Symphony of Creating Creation! WE'RE BLESSED!"

And saying all this, Mark was Aglow and you could hear a pin drop. Before our very eyes Mark had become a Consciously Conscious Human Being of his own Self Guardian Angel, and it was BEAUTIFUL! AND SACRED! AND BIG BIG FUN!

# Twelve

Time passed.

And more Holy Timeless Time passed, then Father James said, "Well, okay, then I do believe—no, I mean I DO KNOW that now is a good time for us to take a break and bring out the *tequila*, and—" he added with a big smile, "we just happened to have purchased your favorite, Victor!"

"*Herradura?*"

"Yes!"

"Oh, wonderful!"

And so we all went into the big main dining room with the large stone fireplace and we drank shots of one of the best *tequilas* ever made, and originally by a Villaseñor. And I now explained to everyone the importance of good *tequila*.

"You see," I said, with my third shot in hand, "*mi papa* explained to me that the only reason the Jews lost the Garden of Eden was because they had no *tequila*. You see, if Adam had had two or three good shots of *Herradura tequila*, instead of that sweet weak Jewish red wine, then when God came down and asked who did it? Who ate the Forbidden fruit from the Tree of Knowledge tree? Adam wouldn't have chickened-out and blamed his wife, and she then wouldn't have blamed that poor snake.

"OH, NO!" I yelled. "Feeling his *tequila,* Adam would've faced God and said, 'I DID IT! ME! *Y QUE?* AND SO WHAT?'

"And God would've been taken back and said, 'Hey, you're feeling pretty frisky today, Adam.'

"And Adam would've said, 'Your damn right, God! Eve and I like it here in the Garden of Eden and we're having a great time!'

"'Well, I'm glad to hear this,' God would've said. Then he would've asked Adam what he was drinking.

"And Adam would've licked his lips and said, '*Tequila* from *Los Altos de Jalisco!*'

"God would've licked his own lips and said, 'You know, Adam, I've never had a shot of *tequila.* Give me one, eh?'

"'Sure, of course, God,' Adam would've said, and God would've loved His shot of *tequila,* and today we'd still all be drinking *tequila* with God in the Garden of Eden! But we aren't, because those poor Jews only had that weak sweet red wine, and so that's why Adam didn't have the guts to speak up and tell God how much THEY LOVED HIS HOLY GARDEN."

Everyone was laughing and laughing with *carcajadas* and we polished off that first bottle, inviting God to join us, then Father James brought out another bottle, and this was when I added the second part of the story that my dad always told me.

"Do you know why they call liquor spirits?' I asked everyone. "Because in the first half of the bottle you find God, but in the second half you find the devil, so I suggest we eat before you open up that another bottle."

Everyone agreed, except the priest who'd had to lie down on the couch.

"Myself," he said, "I'm feeling a whole lot better, so I think one more shot and I'll BE TOTALLY WELL!"

Everyone burst out laughing again, and this was when someone noticed that Joe and *Margarita* had disappeared. They were nowhere to be seen. Then someone spotted them. There they were down by the lake, and they were in each other's arms and the moonlight was sparkling off the lake waters all around them, and tears came to my eyes and most of the nuns, too, and this was when Mary came up and suddenly grabbed me in her arms, turned me around, and kissed me once and twice right on the lips and then she yelled!

"I GOT HIM! I GOT HIM!"

Everyone BURST OUT LAUGHING WITH *CARCAJADAS* AGAIN! And it was WONDERFUL! It was a full moon night, and we'd all ventured into helping to bring Heaven back down to Mother Earth!

# BOOK FOUR

# Thirteen

The next day I was taken back to the airport by the same driver who had picked me up. He asked me how it had gone and I didn't know how to even begin. Finally, I just said, "It went really well, especially this morning, and if we'd been able keep going for a week, we could've reached the levels that my grandmothers reached coming north through the Mexican Revolution of 1910."

"Really?" he said.

"Yes, really," I said.

And he asked no more questions and I was glad, because what could I have said, told him that as a group we'd moved into Our Collective Psychic Powers and we hadn't just "seen" the Future. No, we'd actually manifested the Future just as *Espirito* had done with that waterfall, turning it into a rain of actual gold. Yes, oh, yes, those Nuns and Priests and I had actually become Miracle Makers, and so the Vatican had, indeed, already been relocated to Ireland, and we already had our first woman Pope and she truly was OF JESUS!

Well, actually, she was our second woman Pope, because our first woman Pope had served in total secrecy many centuries ago. And also, I guess, I could've told him that by April 2052 there would be no more wars in the world. Conflicts would be—not negotiated—but dissolved before they could solidify into emotional-manifestation just as that international lawyer who spoke eight languages had explained to me back in 1993 in Portland, Oregon right after we'd returned from Spain.

I was quiet the rest of our drive to the airport and then in Chicago, where I was changing planes, a storm came in and we were told we'd have about a five to six-hour layover. I decided to just relax, find a quiet corner, stretch out on the floor, and take a nap. Up ahead two little girls were running in the aisle and laughing and playing.

"Hi, girls!" I said. They stopped playing. They were about four and five. "I want you young women to Know you are Angels, and you're wonderful, and you came into this world with Total Recall, and so you're in charge, because, you see, your parents have forgotten they're Angels, too, and so you need to re-teach them. Have a good life," I added, tipping my Stetson to them and then kept going.

Up ahead, I found a quiet corner by the huge windows facing the runway of incoming and outgoing planes. I put my backpack down, slipped off my western boots, and put my Stetson on top of them so the colorful boots now looked like a very short cowboy. Then I lay down on the floor, stretched out my arms and legs, closed my eyes, and was just relaxing and going to sleep when I felt a presence to the right of me. I opened my eyes and turned to look and saw that here stood those two little girls with two more little girls and an older boy who was probably about eight years old, and they were just staring at me, and not moving and/or saying anything. Then it came to me.

"Oh, yeah," I said, 'I'd like all of you to Know you are Angels. Beams of Light just like Albert Einstein, and so you came into this world KNOWING EVERYTHING there is to Know! And you are wonderful and fantastic, and your

Angel Voice within you is your Holy Voice of Geniusing, and so you young people are in charge, because your parents have forgotten they are Angels, too, and so you need to re-educate them and let them Know they are wonderful, too. In fact," I added, "you guys still have cellular memory that your arms are really wings. So go ahead, spread out your Angel-Arm-Wings, and go for it!"

And so they did, they spread out their arms and began flying around screeching with joy and *gusto*!

"Wonderful! Great! And now I need to get some sleep, so please just go back to your parents, but don't forget, you're in charge and you're really, really ANGELS AND WONDERFUL!"

They flew around me a couple of more times, and then they flew off and I took in a few deep breaths, put my Stetson over my eyes, and went right off to sleep. And I was dreaming of my horse Casanova and Buccaneer Beach and smelling Wild Flowers when someone kicked the bottom of my left foot. But I just ignored it and kept sleeping until they kicked me again and this kick was much harder. I opened my eyes, took the Stetson off my face, and I saw there was a tall girl just beyond my feet. She was maybe 10 or 11 years old and she was staring at me and all about her were these smaller shorter kids. About 10 of them. And they, too, were just staring at me.

Well, I sat up, brought my water bottle out of my back-pack, drank, then told them the same thing that I'd already said two times before, and when I finished they didn't go away. No, they stayed all around me flapping their arms like wings, and then here came some more kids, and some more, and then I noticed that their parents were coming, too, and when one father grabbed his little four year old girl to take her away, she jerked loose from him with power and yelled, "NO! I'M AN ANGEL!" And she came back to be with the other children with her arms out like wings and her whole face was full of joy!

The father rushed at me. His whole face was red with rage.

"WHO ARE YOU? What have you done to our children!" he shouted.

And I could now see that he wasn't alone. There were about a dozen other parents all staring at me, too. I got up off the floor. I had no idea what to say and/or do. I closed my eyes, rubbed my face, took in a deep breath, and once more I caught the scent of Wild Flowers, and when I opened my eyes here was Jesus with his Sacred Holy Arms outstretched, too, and He was laughing and spinning around and around with the JOY OF A CHILD!

I laughed. His laughter was contagious, but I could also see that this angry father in front of me didn't think that this was a laughing situation.

"Look," I said, still smiling with *gusto*, "I'm a writer and . . . and, well, we're doing research at the University of Houston in conjunction with Harvard on children having Total Recall Of Being Angels. You see, children are nowadays coming into the world with a way more advanced understanding of how the Universe really works than us older people. We adults basically still live in the dark ages of the illusion that the world is flat, time is linear, and that there is separation. But these kids who are now coming into this manifestation of reality Cellularly Know that all of Creation is Interconnected, and so they're not fear-based, and are Free to Be Geniusing Angels as a Way Of

Living. Just look at them, they're so happy, because they Know, just like a rose Knows, how to Be," I said, thinking this explanation would calm him down. But it didn't.

"Do you have proof?" he barked.

"Proof of what?" I asked.

"Proof that you're not a crackpot!"

"Oh, yeah, sure," I said, "in my backpack I have a copy of my National Best Seller *Rain of Gold,* and some great articles written about me in the *New York Times,* the *L.A. Times, Chicago Tribune, People Magazine* and a bunch of others. Here, let me get them out and—"

"No! You don't have to do that! I just want my child to come back with me. You had no right!"

"You mean you're upset that I told your child that she's an Angel and a Genius and Wonderful?"

"Well, no, I'm not offended by that," he said. "I'm offended by her not obeying me and . . . and . . . I don't need to be explaining myself to you. She's my child!"

And I almost said, "Not really. She's God-Goding's child and she's her own Human Angel Person," but I decided this wouldn't be the best thing to say, especially since all the other parents were looking at me with concern, too. So I turned to the kids.

"All right, you Geniusing Angels," I said. "Please, all of you go back to your parents, but remember you're in charge, because you're—"

"My little girl IS NOT IN CHARGE!" yelled the father.

But the mother only laughed. "Oh, come on, honey, you know she is," she said. "Thank you very much," she said, turning to me.

A couple of the kids came up and hugged me, and one little boy put his shoes into my boots, fell over, but then got up and his whole face was in ecstasy as he tried walking off wearing my boots that came up past his knees.

People started laughing.

"Can we get your book at any bookstore?"

"Yeah, sure, of course, and it's a trilogy, *Rain of Gold, 13 Senses*, and *Wild Steps of Heaven*. But the young adult book is *Walking Stars*, a bunch of short stories, and the first one is entitled *The Smartest Human I Ever Met, My Brother's Dog Shep*. Pets are so important for kids. They teach love and caretaking and total responsibility. And check out my children's book. That's where education really begins. Thank you. Thank you very much and I'm sorry if I upset you."

The tall girl stayed behind.

"Yes," I said.

"Thank you," she said. "I just knew that there was more to life."

And saying this she began to glow, then she turned and took off running and so I lay back down, closed my eyes, put my Stetson over my face and went back to sleep. Oh, some of those parents had truly looked all bent out of shape. And who could blame them. Their kids had been Aglow with Light just like that tall girl and they hadn't been able to see it. Only the kids could see and feel each other's Glowing Holy Light of Love*Amor*. Oh, I could hardly wait to get home so I could go across the grass and past the chicken coops to tell my mother what had happened.

MIRACLE MAKERS are we!

DREAMCATCHERS are we!

SONGSHIFTERS are we!

And never in a billion years had I ever expected to go on such a FANTASTIC GHOSTING VOYAGEDREAM OF TOTAL TRANSFORMATION!

It was DONE!

It was COMPLETED!

It was FINISHED IN BEAUTY WITH ABUNDANCE FOR ALL JUST LIKE ON OUR OTHER SIX SISTER PLANETS!

Finally, at long last, we were Awakening Collectively, and starting to have INTELLIGENT LIFE ON THIS PLANET, TOO!

AMEN!

AWOMEN!

ACHILDREN!

# Afterword

Okay, dear reader, the date is now May 30, 2014, my mother's birthday, and she's here with me in my writing room, and yet she passed over in 2000. Also I'd like you to Know that earlier today I went up the hill to the cemetery to visit with her and my father and my brother, telling them that I just finished this book today on her birthday. Immediately a breeze came up and I could smell an Abundance of Wild Flowers, and wild birds were in the trees all about me singing and chirping. My mother had been a bird lover and she'd always put out feeders for the wild ones.

I lay down on the grass and looked up at the beautiful Father Sky and there wasn't a cloud to be seen. I stretched and yawned. I'd been up writing since 3 a.m. and it was now about 2 in the afternoon and I was scheduled to get a massage in about an hour and a half. I loved my life. I hadn't chickened-out and I was now 74 and in great shape and great health and only 4 years away from our Most Perfect Age of 78.

That Inspiring Experience with those Nuns and Priests happened back in 1997 or 1998. I don't remember which. And six months later I was invited to meet with 16 different Christian denominations in Iowa and they were quick and very open to hear and understand, and yet they'd been much slower to allow the information to reach their hearts.

Then, I'll never forget, I'd closed my eyes and asked for guidance and instantly I smelled Wild Flowers and Jesus had come laughing and spinning and dancing into their midst. I'd started laughing and immediately I'd Known with a capital 'K' what to do.

"Please!" I'd said in a loud voice to the 16 ministers. "Let's stop all talking, all thinking, and . . . please, I now need one man and one woman to come up here and be in front with me!"

There were only three women ministers, but all three jumped up and one was really fast and got to me before the others. It was fun seeing them run. But the men, they hadn't even gotten out of their seats yet.

"COME ON!" I YELLED. "GIVE ME A MAN!"

Finally, two got up and the younger one was faster and came to me. I put the woman on my left, the man on my right, held their hands in mine, took in several deep breaths, then spoke.

"Look," I said, "I want you to learn two Mexican words. Wet your lips. Good! Good! *Cariño! Cariño!* Which means being affectionate. And the word *abrazo! Abrazo!* Which means to hug, to embrace. Okay, wet your lips so you can roll those 'R's and repeat *abrazo! Abrazo!* Very good! Very good!

"Okay," I now said, dropping the man's hand and turning to the woman minister, "in the future I never want you to ask anyone 'How are you?' because the truth is you don't want to know, and the second truth is he or she will tell you 'fine', and then they'll ask you and you'll say 'fine', too, and you've just had a very superficial greeting.

"No, in the future, I want you to look at the person in the eyes, because the eyes are the gateway to the Soul. And I want you to then take in a deep breath, look at the pupils of the eyes, seeing deeply into the other person, and then say—not 'have a nice day'. That's lame. You say, 'Have a FANTASTIC DAY AND FABULOUS JUICY NIGHT OF WILD ADVENTUROUS DREAMS!'"

All the ministers started laughing, even the men.

"Then after this," I said, "you move in close to the person, heart to heart, which is, of course, on your left, and you press chest to chest, then bend your knees and wiggle your ass as fast as you can, because wherever the ass goes the brains follow. You've all seen it. Uptight ass means uptight brain. And a relaxed ass means a relaxed brain, and with a relaxed brain you then automatically start accessing your heart, and once you're in your Heart Center, then the Soul Center kicks in."

And this woman minister put her heart to my heart and bent her knees, and oh, how she wiggled her wildly happy relaxed ass right along with me, and people burst out laughing with *CARCAJADAS!* Then I let go of her and turned to the young minister and he turned red-faced, glanced out at everyone like he was asking to please be rescued, but then he turned back to me and he was game, and we did the same ritual, and then wiggled together.

"OKAY!" I shouted. "Now everyone get on your feet with relaxed asses and greet the person to the right of you and the person to the left of you! GO FOR IT! Because wherever the ass goes the brains follow and we've got to get out of our heads and relax our asses so we can access our Hearts, then SLIP-SLIDE INTO OUR SOULS!"

And all this time Jesus was loving it and laughing and spinning and sending His Sacred Holy *Amor* to everyone, and all 16 Christian ministers were now available Heart to Heart and Soul to Soul.

A year later I was invited to meet with a bunch of nuns in Sacramento. Or maybe it was Oakland. I don't remember which. But the point is that they had me meet them at a *Tequila* bar and they were all dressed up to party, and things took off immediately. Then just last year, 2013, I was invited to northern Kentucky right across the river to a church called the Mother of God and I met this most beautiful nun in her early 80s and after my talk, I spoke to her. "Excuse me," I said, "but how would you like to be our first official Woman Pope now that we're scheduled to move to Ireland?"

"Me?" she said. "OH, WHY NOT? SURE, OF COURSE!"

And she'd said it with such confidence and openness that we just started laughing and laughing together.

Oh, I tell you, the whole world is CHANGING SO FAST, and everywhere I go I'm meeting people who are receiving, receiving, receiving the same HOLY INFORMATION that I've been receiving for over 54 years!

Take, for instance, 911 and those two towers.

I was in New York two years before that happened and I told my family that those towers were coming down, because they were totally blocking out the sunlight of that tiny little historical famous church that was only four blocks away.

Greed had totally obstructed the significance of that little beautiful House of God. My eyes had filled with tears and I'd said, "Those towers are coming down!" And they did, and when they did I immediately saw us sending planes full of food and toys and tools and blankets and tents and fresh pure water to all the people from where those "terrorists" had come, and then the people of people for the people of that region would rejoice and bring their own radicals into Harmony and Peace.

And I've now met five people who also Knew that those towers were coming down and they also had a DreamVoyage of us sending planes full of food and toys and tools and clean water and medical supplies! And why did these people KNOW THIS?! BECAUSE WE'RE ALL INTERPLANETARY CONNECTED and this is how our Cousins on our Six Sister Planets did it!

YOU KNOW IT!

I KNOW IT!

WE ALL KNOW IT!

AND ESPECIALLY ALL THESE YOUNG KIDS KNOW IT WHO ARE NOW COMING INTO MANIFESTATION!

War is out of date!

Revenge is out of date!

Judgment is out of date!

Compassion is OUR MODERN TOOL!

Forgiveness is OUR MODERN TOOL!

AND OPEN HEARTED KINDNESS IS OUR GREATEST MODERN TOOL!

And I had a dream of OVER A MILLION Snow Goose Global Thanksgiving locations by November 2026 and all these people were feeding the masses, and when an elderly woman said to the server, "Oh, what a beautiful jacket-blouse. My mother used to have one like that." The elegantly dressed server said, "It is yours, my sister!" And she slipped of her gorgeous jacket-blouse without embarrassment, and continued serving in her bra and apron.

And everyone saw her start to Glow with the Light of God-Goding for she'd become OF JESUS! OF BUDDHA! OF MOHAMMAD! OF ALL HUMAN HEART AND SOUL!

I awoke crying and laughing, I was so happy. BIG BIG HAPPY!

And I met Obama 20-some years ago in South Chicago just off 19th Street through Mary Gonzales and Greg, the ex-Jesuit, and I saw how he settled a dispute between Blacks and Latinos by INSPIRING both sides to UNITY WITH JOY!

And so I told that skinny young guy with big ears he was going to be President of the United States for two terms, and yet his greatest work would be after he got out of the confines of the Oval Office.

He started arguing with me, telling me that it couldn't happen, because you had to come from a large state like Texas, New York, or California that had lots of delegates, or be independently wealthy like the Kennedys. Finally, I got angry and said, "STOP ARGUING AND START PREPARING! It's done! It's finished! And written in the stars!"

And so thusly I say to all of you, just listen to this New Last Pope. He's a Jesuit. He's from the New World. He lives in an apartment, refusing to live in the Vatican. And you will Know deep inside your Heart and Soul that he is TOTALLY OF JESUS! And so, of course, he's endorsing the whole definition Of Being Catholic: universal, all-inclusive; of general interest and value; hence, having broad sympathies and understanding; liberal.

SO STOP ARGUING! And start preparing FOR WORLDWIDE HARMONY AND PEACE AND ABUNDANCE FOR ALL!

IT'S DONE!

IT'S COMPLETED!

IT'S ALREADY WRITTEN IN THE STARS!

# Our Global Interplanetary Musical

Of Our United Global Harmonic Birthing Of Goding for 13 Full Mother Moons every 100 years starting with Enya calling, calling, calling with Gratitude Of Our Snow Geese Angels Of Our Human Selves from Our Mother Of God Church Of Ireland to Our Grand Pyramids Of Mexico, then the Philippines, an Interplanetary Musical in Cosmic Frequency, Of Our Consciously Consciousness Of Our Symphony Of Creation Creating OF OUR HOLY SACRED BIRTHING OF OUR ALMIGHTY CREATOR!

ACHILDREN!

AWOMEN!

AMEN!

Hail Our Holy Lady Of Goding New Pope along with Her Cardinals and Bishops and Priests and Sisters from every House Of Worship around and around Our Whole Mother Earth, We Unite with Our 100s of 1,000,000s of Angels in JOY, and it is now FINISHED!

COMPLETED!

DONE! In conjunction with Our Six Sister Planets, and hence Already Written In Our Beloved *Familia De Nuestras Estrellas!*

# Trilogy

About the two other volumes of the trilogy *Revenge of a Catholic Schoolboy*, the second one is titled *Walking in Beauty* and it will start with a leap from this event of the nuns and priests to other happenings, and especially go into the Global Design of doing Acupuncture to our Mother Earth in order to start helping her heal.

Then volume three, *Dancing Stars*, will reconnect us with our Star Cousins from our Six Sister Planets through the No Talk Cafés where every third person you meet will most likely be one of our Cousins who SongShifted into a recognizable Human Form. You see, World-Wide Harmony and Peace and ABUNDANCE FOR ALL ARE IN THE BAG! There's nothing we can do to stop it!

Thank you, *gracias*, we're finally on our way Back To The Future!

Victor E. Villaseñor

P.S. Also, note that these No Talk Cafés will open up in Mexico City, Los Angeles, New York, Dallas, Chicago, Seattle, then go Global, and 90% of all profits will be used for World-Wise Education focused on our Interplanetary Concepts of Harmony, Peace, and Abundance for All!

Made in the USA
San Bernardino, CA
27 January 2015